Supreme Court Justices
in the Post-Bork Era

Teaching Texts in Law and Politics

David A. Schultz
General Editor

Vol. 21

PETER LANG
New York • Washington, D.C./Baltimore • Bern
Frankfurt am Main • Berlin • Brussels • Vienna • Oxford

Joyce A. Baugh

Supreme Court Justices in the Post-Bork Era

Confirmation Politics and Judicial Performance

PETER LANG
New York • Washington, D.C./Baltimore • Bern
Frankfurt am Main • Berlin • Brussels • Vienna • Oxford

Library of Congress Cataloging-in-Publication Data

Baugh, Joyce A.
Supreme Court justices in the post-Bork era: confirmation politics
and judicial performance / Joyce A. Baugh.
p. cm. — (Teaching texts in law and politics; vol. 21)
Includes bibliographical references and index.
1. Judges—Selection and appointment—Political aspects—United States.
2 Political questions and judicial power—United States. 3 Judicial process—United
States. 4. United States. Supreme Court. I Title. II. Series.
KF8776.B38   347.73'2634—dc21   2001034685
ISBN 0-8204-5683-7
ISSN 1083-3447

Die Deutsche Bibliothek-CIP-Einheitsaufnahme

Baugh, Joyce A.:
Supreme court justices in the post-bork era: confirmation politics and judicial
performance / Joyce A. Baugh.–New York; Washington, D.C./Baltimore; Bern;
Frankfurt am Main; Berlin; Brussels; Vienna; Oxford: Lang.
(Teaching texts in law and politics; Vol. 21)
ISBN 0-8204-5683-7
NE: GT

Cover design by Joni Holst

The paper in this book meets the guidelines for permanence and durability
of the Committee on Production Guidelines for Book Longevity
of the Council of Library Resources.

Printed in the United States of America

Contents

Acknowledgments   vii

Introduction   1

Chapter 1   The Bork Confirmation Controversy   6
Chapter 2   David Souter: "A Home-Run for Conservatives?"   18
Chapter 3   Clarence Thomas: Dependable Conservative   40
Chapter 4   Ruth Bader Ginsburg: "A Judge's Judge and a Lawyer's Lawyer"   61
Chapter 5   Stephen Breyer: Pragmatic Moderate   81
Chapter 6   Conclusion   101

Name/Subject Index   121

Court Case Index   127

Acknowledgments

I wish to acknowledge a number of individuals for assistance in making this book possible.

I would like to thank Thomas R. Hensley of Kent State University and Christopher E. Smith of Michigan State University, my collaborators on previous projects on the Supreme Court and its justices, for their continued encouragement and advice.

Central Michigan University, by means of a university research professor leave, provided me with the time to work on this book. I also would like to recognize my colleague, John H. Dinse, for his dedicated service as acting chair of the Department of Political Science in my absence.

Special thanks go to Phyllis Korper, editor, and Lisa Dillon, production manager, at Peter Lang Publishing for their assistance and support in completing this project. I also am grateful to Professor David Schultz, series editor, for his helpful comments and insights, particularly in the early stages of the book.

Finally, my husband, Roger D. Hatch, deserves special recognition. He contributed his excellent editing skills to the manuscript, and his love, patience, and unwavering support helped to sustain me as I worked to complete this book.

Introduction

The appointment of justices to the United States Supreme Court has always been a topic of considerable interest to academics, legal observers, and the media. This especially has been true since the controversial nomination of federal appeals court judge Robert Bork in 1987. Since the appointment of Stephen Breyer in 1994, there has been no vacancy on the Court, and the assumption is that George W. Bush may have the opportunity to appoint as many as three justices. For several years, rumors in political and legal circles have suggested that Chief Justice William Rehnquist and Justice Sandra Day O'Connor are interested in retiring but have been hoping to time their departures so that their successors could be named by a Republican president. Some also have mentioned that Justice John Paul Stevens, the oldest of the sitting justices, may retire in the near future.

Supreme Court observers continually have speculated about whether future nominations would be marked by the rancor and controversy that characterized the Bork (and subsequent Clarence Thomas) confirmations. Immediately after the Bork nomination was defeated in 1987, critics claimed that the confirmation process had become politicized. They downplayed the role of politics in President Reagan's selection of Bork and blamed liberal interest groups and liberal senators for the acrimonious proceedings. Such claims about the new "politicization" of the process were overblown, however. In his comprehensive study of Supreme Court appointments beginning with George Washington's administration, Henry Abraham presents strong evidence that politics always has played an important role in the appointment of Supreme Court justices. He discussed several factors that affect presidential selection of nominees: (1) objective merit (2) personal friendship (3) balancing representation or representativeness on the Court, and (4) political and ideological compatibility. He concludes that political and ideological compatibility has been "the controlling factor."[1]

Despite clear evidence of the long-term role of politics in Supreme Court appointments, claims about the politicization of the process were widespread, and a task force was established to examine the process and propose reforms. In its report issued in 1988, the Twentieth Century Fund suggested these reforms: (1) limits on the number of participants in the confirmation hearings, (2) preventing nominees from testifying at confirmation hearings, (3) if nominees testify, preventing senators from asking questions regarding how they would deal with specific issues, and (4) basing confirmation decisions on nominees' written records and testimony from legal experts.[2] Other legal experts offered additional reform proposals, including having the nominees testify immediately upon the nomination and delaying testimony from others, prohibiting testimony from groups, prohibiting televised hearings, banning public hearings, and doing away with hearings altogether.[3]

The controversy over the Bork nomination (and the Thomas confirmation in 1991) generated a proliferation of publications analyzing the Supreme Court appointment process. In *The Confirmation Mess,* Stephen Carter examined several high-profile nominations for appointments to federal office, giving particular attention to Bork and Thomas. Carter decried the system of confirming nominees for federal office as one "in which strategy (especially public relations strategy) is far more important than issues or qualifications."[4] While recognizing that "vicious confirmation battles" are not a new phenomenon, he alleged that the proceedings are "rougher" today because televised hearings have transformed these events from "inside-the-Beltway rituals into full-blown national extravaganzas."[5] Carter concluded by critiquing various proposals to reform the process. He rejected most of these as ineffective in really improving things: prohibiting confirmation hearings from being televised; closing the confirmation hearings or discontinuing them; discontinuing testimony from nominees; and prohibiting testimony from interest groups. As better alternatives, he advanced proposals that would require constitutional amendments, including changing the vote necessary for confirmation from a simple majority to a 2/3 vote, imposing term limits for Supreme Court justices, and electing Supreme Court justices.[6]

Mark Silverstein, in *Judicious Choices: The New Politics of Supreme Court Confirmations,* maintained that the appointment process changed in a dramatic way long before the Bork episode, with Lyndon Johnson's failed nomination of Abe Fortas for chief justice in 1968. He attributed the increased contentiousness of the process to systemic factors, including changes in the nature of judicial power, the changing roles of the national parties, and changes in the structure and operation of the Senate. According to Silverstein, as the Supreme Court increasingly issued decisions to protect civil liberties and civil rights, progressives turned to the federal judiciary to protect their interests. This in turn had profound effects on the selection of Supreme Court justices.

The litigation victories of the New Progressives in turn hastened the emergence of the New Right in the Republican Party and gave rise to intense scrutiny of judicial appointments by powerful forces in both parties. The changes in the nature of judicial power over the last three decades ratcheted the stakes still higher by making the federal judiciary amenable to a wider range of litigants and claims. . . . Changes in the formal rules and institutional folkways of the Senate enhanced the influence of individual senators at the expense of institutional cohesion and leadership control. By the late 1960s these developments converged, making public battles over staffing the Supreme Court almost inevitable.[7]

In *Shaping America: The Politics of Supreme Court Appointments,* George Watson and John Stookey acknowledged that the selection of Supreme Court justices inevitably is a political, ideological, and controversial process, but, in contrast to some other commentators, they do not find this problematic. In fact, they suggested that it *should* be this way, given the critical role the Court plays in deciding important policy questions. Watson and Stookey argued that both presidents and senators recognize the political nature and implications of Supreme Court appointments and that they simply should be honest about this.

> Who is on the Court is an important political question. Explicit political conflict about a nominee should be considered legitimate and appropriate. Senators should not ignore questions of ethics, competency, or temperament, but they should be encouraged to jettison attempts to wrap their support or opposition in these terms if in fact their objections are grounded in political and ideological objections. . . . [A]n explicitly political process would, we believe, actually civilize the nomination process.[8]

John Anthony Maltese, in *The Selling of Supreme Court Nominees,* also accepted the inevitability of the political nature of the Supreme Court appointment process. Beginning with George Washington's nomination of Associate Justice John Rutledge for Chief Justice in 1795, Maltese demonstrated that there have been controversial nominations throughout American history. Other examples from the late nineteenth and early twentieth century included Rutherford B. Hayes's nomination of Stanley Matthews in 1881, Woodrow Wilson's nomination of Louis Brandeis in 1916, and Herbert Hoover's nomination of Associate Justice Charles Evans Hughes for Chief Justice in 1930. Through examination of these appointments, along with in-depth case studies of the failed nominations of John Parker in 1890 and Clement Haynesworth, Jr. in 1969, Maltese demonstrated that partisan politics and interest group influence in Supreme Court appointments did not begin in 1987 with the nomination of Bork. Like Silverstein, he emphasized that the process has become more political over time because of important changes in the political system. He pointed to the emergence of interest groups in the appointment process, rule changes in the Senate that opened debate on nominations, and the ability of interest groups to have a greater influence on senators as a result of direct election. Maltese's major thesis is that the process now requires the "selling" of nominees.

> [W]hat is different about today's appointment process is not its politicization but the range of players in the process and the techniques of politicization that they use. Today's confirmation battles are no longer government affairs between the president and the Senate; they are public affairs, open to a broad range of players. Thus, overt lobbying, public opinion polls, advertising campaigns, focus groups, and public appeals have all become a routine part of the process.[9]

Clearly the Bork nomination was not the first controversial Supreme Court appointment, but it certainly seemed unprecedented in terms of the level of attention and participation it generated. Senators engaged in greater scrutiny and questioning of a nominee than ever before, and the number of interest groups participating in the process reached an all-time high. The hearings lasted twelve days, with nearly five days of testimony from the nominee himself, and, in the end, senators rejected his confirmation by the largest margin in history.

Scholars and other commentators from across the political spectrum have predicted that the Bork controversy would have a long-lasting impact on the appointment process in two important ways. First, Supreme Court nominations in the future would be marked by a significant increase in both media attention and interest group participation. Second, and perhaps more importantly, observers predicted that presidents would be more likely to appoint either "stealth" nominees—that is, individuals who share their ideological perspectives but lack a "paper trail" of controversial writings and speeches—or judicial moderates who would be less likely to evoke serious opposition from those on either side of the political and ideological spectrum.

This study examines these predictions about the impact of the Bork controversy by focusing on the four subsequent nominations to the Supreme Court: David Souter, Clarence Thomas, Ruth Bader Ginsburg, and Stephen Breyer. The study examines the nomination and confirmation process for each of these justices and also looks at their subsequent performance on the Court. Have they been judicial moderates, or have they demonstrated ideological consistency in either a conservative or liberal direction? The first chapter discusses the Bork nomination controversy in more detail. The next four chapters focus on each of the four subsequent nominees in order of their appointment to the Court. A concluding chapter offers speculation about the future of Supreme Court nominations, considered in light of current power dynamics in the U.S. Senate. At the beginning of George W. Bush's term as president in January 2001, the Senate was equally divided, with Vice President Dick Cheney in a position to cast tie-breaking votes. Questions immediately arose about the types of nominees that Bush would select under these circumstances. Four months later, however, Republican Senator James Jeffords of

Vermont announced that he was leaving the party to become an Independent. Subsequently, Jeffords joined the Democratic caucus, providing Democrats with a working majority and, most importantly for this study, control of the Senate Judiciary Committee. This new scenario makes speculation about the future all the more interesting to observers of the Supreme Court appointment process.

CHAPTER ONE

The Bork Confirmation Controversy

On June 26, 1987, the final day of the 1986–1987 term, Associate Justice Lewis Powell announced his retirement from the Supreme Court. During his fifteen-year tenure, Powell had earned a reputation as a moderate, "swing voter" on the high court. Although Janet Blasecki's comprehensive study of Powell's voting record indicates that he most often was aligned with the Court's conservatives,[1] Powell was viewed as a moderate because in landmark cases he often cast the decisive vote for both conservative and liberal outcomes. For example, he joined the conservatives in creating a "good-faith exception" to the Fourth Amendment exclusionary rule, in limiting the power of federal judges to issue broad busing orders to remedy metropolitan school desegregation, and in upholding a state's property tax scheme of school financing over claims that the resulting disparities violated the Equal Protection Clause.[2] On the other hand, Powell voted with the liberals in striking down policies that denied public education to the children of illegal aliens, that provided public funds for religious schools, and that permitted "victim impact statements" to be used in sentencing decisions in capital cases.[3]

Of particular interest to Court observers was Powell's position on abortion. He was a member of the original *Roe v. Wade* majority, and in subsequent cases he consistently voted to uphold this precedent.[4] Powell also played a pivotal role as author of the controlling opinion in a number of major cases, most notably, the *Bakke* affirmative action case. In *Bakke,* the justices were split 4–4 over the validity of a medical school's admissions program which had set aside a specific number of seats for minority and disadvantaged applicants. In the controlling opinion, Powell, finding a middle ground, held that a strict quota was invalid, but that race could be considered as a factor in admissions decisions.[5]

While the selection of a new justice is always a subject of great interest, Powell's reputation and the dynamics on the Court made this nomination one of extra significance. Only a year earlier, Chief Justice Warren Burger had retired, Associate

Justice William Rehnquist was selected to succeed him, and Antonin Scalia was appointed to fill Rehnquist's seat. While those nominations were not completely without controversy, the Court's ideological balance was not altered because conservative justices were succeeded by conservatives. With Powell's retirement, however, it was clear that the new appointee would tip the balance on the closely divided Court.

The nomination drew attention from activists and interest groups on both the left and right. Conservatives assumed that President Reagan would appoint a justice who would help to form a majority that would finally overturn what they considered to be the liberal excesses of the Warren and Burger Court eras. Liberals were determined to keep a strong conservative off the Court in order to preserve important precedents in such areas as abortion, the First Amendment, criminal procedure, voting rights, and affirmative action.

The Selection of Robert Bork

Reagan administration officials struggled over who the president should select to fill Powell's seat. Federal appeals court judge Robert Bork was championed by conservatives in the Justice Department, particularly Attorney General Edwin Meese, Assistant Attorney General William Bradford Reynolds, and their immediate subordinates. Conservatives believed that a Bork nomination was overdue and that Bork, rather than Antonin Scalia, should have been the choice a year earlier.[6] In fact, as early as 1975, conservatives had suggested Bork as a nominee when President Gerald Ford selected federal appellate judge John Paul Stevens to succeed Justice William O. Douglas.[7] By contrast, the more moderate members of the White House staff, including Chief of Staff Howard Baker, White House Counsel Arthur B. Culvahouse, and Communications Director Thomas Griscom, were of a different mind. They were concerned that Bork's well-established record as a hard-line conservative would create a confirmation battle that the administration needed to avoid.[8] The conservatives prevailed, however, and on July 1, 1987, President Reagan announced Robert Bork as his nominee to fill the vacant seat. At the time, Bork was serving on the federal court of appeals for the District of Columbia circuit, to which he had been appointed in 1982. This court is regarded by many legal experts as the second most important court in the nation because of its role in handling important administrative law matters regarding federal agencies.

Bork's Background

Robert Bork, the son of a steel company purchasing agent and an English teacher, was born in Pittsburgh, Pennsylvania on March 1, 1927. He attended

Pittsburgh public schools until his senior year, when his parents enrolled him in an exclusive prep school in Connecticut. Although Bork eventually became a leading advocate of free market conservatism, as a teenager he was interested in socialism as a result of reading a Marxist analysis of capitalism. After graduating from high school, Bork joined the Marine Corps shortly before the end of World War II. He served for two years and subsequently entered the University of Chicago, where he earned his bachelor's degree in 1948. Following his undergraduate studies, Bork entered the University of Chicago Law School, but his legal education was interrupted when he was called to service as a Marine reserve at the outbreak of the Korean War. He served as a first lieutenant from 1950 to 1952, then returned to Chicago to continue his legal education, completing his J.D. in 1953. During his last year of law school, Bork's philosophy began to shift away from socialism due to the influence of one of his professors who advocated free-market conservatism. After receiving his law degree, Bork worked for one year as a research associate at the University of Chicago Law School before going to work in private practice, first in New York and then in Chicago. He developed a specialty in antitrust law. In 1962, he joined the faculty at Yale Law School, where he initially taught antitrust law and later added courses in constitutional law. His political philosophy continued to develop during this time. Bork, an earlier supporter of Democratic presidential candidates, supported conservative Republican Barry Goldwater for president in 1964. He was one of few faculty members at Yale to do so publicly. Bork's writings during his early years at Yale generally reflected libertarian principles, but by the late 1960s and early 1970s, as American society became increasingly conservative, his philosophy changed from libertarian to social conservative.[9]

As Bork developed a specialty in constitutional law, he rejected the expansive interpretation of the Constitution that had been the hallmark of the Warren Court. He eventually espoused an approach of original intent, which emphasizes that the provisions of the Constitution must be interpreted according to the intentions of the framers.[10] According to its advocates, the original intent approach is necessary to prevent judges from "making law," which is the proper purview of legislators and executives. The philosophy of original intent, or originalism, as the proper method of constitutional interpretation became a subject of great debate and controversy during the early- to mid-1980s. One of its most well-known proponents was Reagan Attorney General Edwin Meese, who became engaged in a debate with Justice William Brennan over the appropriateness of original intent as a method of constitutional interpretation.[11] Those who adhere to originalism insist that it is neutral and nonpolitical, but this approach generally supports conservative positions on constitutional issues.[12] Thus advocates of original intent are highly critical of liberal precedents established in Supreme Court decisions during the Warren and, to a lesser extent, Burger eras.

Bork's writings captured the attention of conservatives in the Nixon Administration, who also were disturbed by the Court's decisions in a number of areas. In fact, President Nixon had campaigned on the theme of appointing "law and order" justices who would overrule the liberal precedents that, in the view of conservatives, were destroying the fabric of American society. Early in Nixon's second term in 1973, Bork was nominated to become United States Solicitor General. Only two months after being appointed as the federal government's top attorney, he gained notoriety for his participation in the infamous "Saturday Night Massacre." Attorney General Elliott Richardson and Deputy Attorney General William Ruckelshaus both refused to follow President Nixon's order to fire Archibald Cox, the special prosecutor investigating the Watergate affair. After their resignations, Bork agreed to serve as acting attorney general and carried out the order.[13]

Bork served as solicitor general until January of 1977, when, following Jimmy Carter's presidential victory, he again joined the faculty of Yale Law School. Four years later, he returned to private practice, becoming a senior partner in the Washington office of his old Chicago firm. His private practice work was short-lived, however, as President Reagan nominated him for a judgeship on the D.C. Circuit Court in 1982. He received the ABA's highest rating and was confirmed by the Senate with a unanimous vote.[14]

On the D.C. Circuit, Bork developed a reputation as a strong conservative judge. His opinions on the appellate court sometimes contained sharp criticisms of Supreme Court precedents, although his record in this regard was not as extensive as his other writings and speeches.

The Controversy Begins

Within a few hours after President Reagan announced Judge Bork's nomination to the high court, Senator Edward Kennedy of Massachusetts delivered a sharp attack on Bork in a speech on the floor of the Senate.

> Robert Bork's America is a land in which women would be forced into back alley abortions, blacks would sit at segregated lunch counters, rogue police could break down citizens' doors in midnight raids, school children could not be taught about evolution, writers and artists could be censored at the whim of government, and the doors of the federal courts would be shut on the fingers of millions of citizens for whom the judiciary is—and is often the only—protector of the individual rights that are the heart of our democracy.
>
> [I]n the current delicate balance of the Supreme Court, his rigid ideology will tip the scales of justice against the kind of country America is and ought to be.[15]

In addition, shortly after the nomination was announced, liberal interest groups sprang into action to block the confirmation. Under the leadership of Ralph Neas, director of the Leadership Conference on Civil Rights, activists mobilized for an all-out, no-holds-barred campaign to persuade the Senate to reject Bork. Over 150 groups representing a variety of interests took part in this effort that began well before the confirmation hearings and continued until the nomination was defeated. This included such well-known civil rights groups and labor organizations as the National Council of Churches, NAACP Legal Defense and Educational Fund, American Civil Liberties Union, the Urban League, National Education Association, United Auto Workers, AFL-CIO, National Council of La Raza, National Organization for Women, and People for the American Way. Despite their disagreements over specific issues, the leaders of these groups set aside their differences to unite in opposition to Bork's confirmation. Instead of engaging in traditional public protests and demonstrations, these activists used a sophisticated media strategy involving targeted radio announcements, video news releases, and newspaper advertising. The idea was to influence the constituencies of key senators to oppose Bork, and these constituents then could pressure their leaders to vote against confirmation.[16]

Bork's opponents characterized him as an extremist, out-of-the-mainstream judge who was out of step with basic American values, but the Reagan administration sought to recast him as a moderate with impeccable credentials for service on the high court. This strategy was developed by the moderate wing of the administration, particularly members of the White House staff, against the wishes of the Justice Department conservatives. The moderates believed that two groups of senators were the key to Bork's confirmation: conservative southern Democrats and moderate northern Republicans. In their view, these senators "had to be told of Bork's credentials, of his deference toward legislators, of his mainstream and distinguished career as a federal judge, one never reversed by the Supreme Court. In other words, Bork's strong association with the right had to be played down and his stature within the legal profession played up."[17] A major problem, however, was Bork's rating from the American Bar Association's Standing Committee on the Federal Judiciary. On a fifteen person-committee, ten members gave him the highest rating of "well-qualified," four concluded he was "not qualified," and one voted "not opposed." Reagan administration officials and sympathetic senators responded by arguing that the "not qualified" votes should be discounted because they were given by four liberals who simply were opposed to Bork's views. They also noted that in his nomination to the federal appeals court a few years earlier the ABA committee unanimously had rated him "well qualified." Committee members justified the change as the result of different qualifications appropriate for lower court judges and Supreme Court justices.[18]

The Confirmation Hearings and Final Vote

Although the Reagan conservatives had hoped for quick action on the nomination once it was announced on July 1, the confirmation hearings before the Senate
Judiciary Committee did not begin until September 15. Senate Judiciary Committee Chairman Joseph Biden was heavily criticized for the delay, but he contended
that senators needed time to examine Bork's extensive record, and they did not
want to spend time on the hearings during the month of August.[19] When the
hearings finally began, Bork testified for nearly five days. Two of his earliest writings, a 1963 *New Republic* article and a series of lectures published in the *Indiana
Law Journal* in 1971, figured prominently in the questioning. In the *New Republic*
article Bork had criticized the public accommodations section of the proposed
Civil Rights Act of 1964 as a violation of the rights of white business owners.

> The discussion we ought to hear is of the cost in freedom that must be paid for such legis-
> lation, the morality of enforcing morals through law, and the likely consequences for law
> enforcement of trying to do so. . . . Of the ugliness of racial discrimination there need be
> no argument. . . . But it is one thing when stubborn people express their racial antipathies
> in laws which prevent individuals, whether white or Negro, from dealing with those who
> are willing to deal with them, and quite another to tell them that even as individuals they
> may not act on their racial preferences in particular areas of life. The principle of such leg-
> islation is that if I find your behavior ugly by my standards, moral or aesthetic, and if you
> proved stubborn about adopting my view of the situation, I am justified in having the state
> coerce you into more righteous paths. That is itself a principle of unsurpassed ugliness.[20]

In the *Indiana Law Review* article Bork articulated his approach to constitutional interpretation. He emphasized that the Constitution protects rights only if
they are addressed explicitly in that document. If not, Bork said that judges must
leave these matters to legislatures to decide. He was especially critical of the
Court's 1965 decision in *Griswold v. Connecticut,* which established a constitutional right of privacy. In addition, he advocated a narrow view of the First
Amendment's free speech clause, asserting that only political speech is worthy of
constitutional protection.[21]

Despite his strong conservative record, in his opening statement, Bork described himself as a moderate, and he expressed his eagerness to share his views
with the Committee.

> My philosophy of judging, Mr. Chairman, as you pointed out, is neither liberal nor con-
> servative. It is simply a philosophy of judging which gives the Constitution a full and fair
> interpretation but, where the Constitution is silent, leaves the policy struggles to the Con-
> gress, the President, the legislatures and executives of the 50 States, and to the American
> people.
>
> I welcome the opportunity to come before the committee and answer whatever ques-
> tions the members may have. I am quite willing to discuss with you my judicial philosophy

and the approach I take to deciding cases. I cannot, of course, commit myself as to how I might vote on any particular case and I know you would not wish me to do that.[22]

Bork was questioned about his views on a range of topics, including his philosophy of constitutional interpretation, the role of precedent, and various civil rights and liberties issues. While a significant portion of the questioning focused on the two articles described earlier, senators noted that Bork continued to express some of those views long after the articles were written, even after his appointment to the federal bench in 1982.

Seeking to reconcile his earlier statements with his claim of being a moderate who had no ideological agenda, Bork sometimes told the Committee that he was simply engaging in an academic debate. For example:

SENATOR THURMOND. Judge Bork, much of the criticism lodged against you stems from articles and speeches attributed to you over the years which are critical of various rulings of the Supreme Court. Do you feel any distinction should be drawn between your private writings and any responsibilities you would have as a Supreme Court Justice?

JUDGE BORK. As a professor, I felt free to—and indeed was encouraged to—engage in theoretical discussion. I primarily aimed my writing at Supreme Court decisions which I thought were not adequately explained—and explanation is the heart of judging. As a judge, you cannot be as speculative.[23]

Furthermore, in his previous speeches and writings, Bork maintained that judges should feel free to reverse Supreme Court precedents that they believe were incorrectly decided. In a 1985 speech, he said:

I don't think that in the field of constitutional law, precedent is all that important. And I say that for two reasons. One is historical and traditional. The court has never thought constitutional precedent was all that important—the reason being that if you construe a statute incorrectly, the Congress can pass a law and correct you. If you construe the Constitution incorrectly, Congress is helpless. You're the final word. And if you become convinced that a prior court has misread the Constitution, I think it's your duty to go back and correct it.[24]

And just six months before being nominated to the high court, in a speech before the Federalist Society, Bork expressed similar sentiments. "Certainly at the least, I would think [an] originality judge would have no problem whatever in overruling a non-originality precedent, because that precedent by the very basis of his judicial philosophy, has no legitimacy. It comes from nothing the framers intended."[25] In his opening statement, however, Bork backed away from these strong statements.

[A] judge must have great respect for precedent. It is one thing as a legal theorist to criticize the reasoning of a prior decision, even to criticize it severely, as I have done. It is another and more serious thing altogether for a judge to ignore or overturn a prior decision. That requires such careful thought.

Times come, of course, when even a venerable precedent can and should be over-ruled. . . .

Nevertheless, overruling should be done sparingly and cautiously. Respect for precedent is part of the great tradition of our law, just as is fidelity to the intent of those who ratified the Constitution and enacted our statutes.[26]

In backing away from his earlier claims, he argued that some decisions, no matter how badly reasoned, were long-settled and should not be disturbed.

[I]f it [a prior decision] is wrongly decided—and you have to give respect to your predecessors' judgment on these matters—the presumption against overruling remains, because it may be that there are private expectations built up on the basis of the prior decision. It may be that governmental and private institutions have grown up around that prior decision. There is a need for stability and continuity in the law. There is a need for predictability in legal doctrines.[27]

In response to some questions about his prior statements, Bork said that he had changed his views on some issues. For example, Senator Strom Thurmond asked if he adhered to his earlier position that the First Amendment should be interpreted narrowly, to protect only political speech. Bork replied:

Well, Senator, I should point out I am a little surprised that what was an academic exercise and engaging in a debate and trying out a theory has become somehow the core of my philosophy. The article itself said at the end that these remarks are intended to be tentative and exploratory. At the moment, I do not see how I can avoid them.

My views have changed for the simple reason—I was looking for a bright-line test by which judges could decide which speech was protected and which was not. I have since become persuaded—in fact, I was persuaded . . . that the bright-line made no sense; it would be impossible to follow. . . .

So my bright-line eroded, and I now think—I have for some time—first amendment protection applies to moral discourse, it applies to scientific speech, it applies to news, it applies to opinion, it applies to literature.[28]

One of the most heated exchanges occurred when Senator Kennedy questioned Bork about his earlier criticism of the public accommodations provisions of the Civil Rights Act of 1964.

SENATOR KENNEDY. Given the two articles which you offered in 1963 and in 1964, when did you first publicly change your position on the Civil Rights Act?

JUDGE BORK. I do not know if I did it in the classroom or not, I know that the first time–

SENATOR KENNEDY. Publicly, you have written two important declarations. I think we are entitled to know if you were prepared to make those comments in public. I would be interested in when you made some public comment or statement. . . . I would be interested in when you might be able to indicate to us that you changed your position on the Civil Rights Act.

JUDGE BORK. Well I think it is implicit in some of the things that I wrote earlier, but I first said it, I think, where it was written down at least, in a confirmation hearing in 1973.

Bork attempted to deflect additional criticism by pointing out his enforcement of rights for minorities when he was solicitor general and his shift away from libertarian principles that had influenced his opposition to the Civil Rights Act. Kennedy then criticized him for taking so long to repudiate publicly his earlier statements. The exchange continued.

JUDGE BORK. Senator, I do not usually keep issuing my new opinions every time I change my mind. I just do not. . . .

SENATOR KENNEDY. The point that I would make here is that you felt it was sufficiently important to publish your views at a time when we were having a national debate in the early part of the 1960's on civil rights legislation. We were having a national debate in 1968 on the whole issue of fair housing. We were having a national debate in 1972 on other civil rights legislation and you did not feel . . . sufficiently aroused in terms of your altered or changed views, that you were prepared to publish those views. I would just say I wish you had been as quick to publicize your change of heart as you were to broadcast your opposition.[29]

The issue of whether the Equal Protection Clause should apply to gender discrimination was another area of concern for some senators. Bork previously had said that the Clause never should have been extended beyond racial discrimination. He appeared to soften his position here as well.

At the time I wrote about the equal protection clause, the Court had never extended the clause to women. But in addition to that . . . the Court was in the process of saying it applies to blacks, it applies to illegitimate children, it applies to somebody else, and they were picking groups—which I thought was a wrong way to apply it. I think you apply it by requiring a reasonable basis for any distinction made between individuals or groups. . . .

In the case of gender, it will depend on the particular issue. . . . But in that sense, requiring a reasonable basis for any distinction made—yes, the clause applies to women; it applies to every person.[30]

On the issue of the constitutional right of privacy and the *Griswold* case, Bork adhered more closely to his original claims, but even here his language was less strident. Both in the *Indiana Law Journal* article and on later occasions Bork had criticized the decision as an example of judges imposing their own values to create constitutional rights rather than deferring to the legislature to make decisions over competing values. Senator Biden pressed him on this:

THE CHAIRMAN. [Y]ou suggest that unless the Constitution, I believe in the past you used the phrase, textually identifies a value that is worthy of being protected, then competing values in society, the competing value of a public utility, in the example you used, to go out and make money—that economic right has no more or less constitutional protection than the right of a married couple to use or not use birth control in their bedroom. Is that what you are saying?

JUDGE BORK. No, I am not entirely, but I will straighten it out. I was objecting to the way Justice Douglas, in that opinion, *Griswold v. Connecticut,* derived this right. It may be possible to derive an objection to an anti-contraceptive statute in some other way. I do not know.[31]

Bork emphasized again that decisions over these competing values should be left to legislatures, not to judges. Senators Biden and Kennedy kept asking whether he believed that a constitutional right of privacy exists. He continued to be critical of *Griswold* but did not clearly answer the question.

SENATOR KENNEDY. As I hear you, you do not believe that there is a general right of privacy that is in the Constitution.

JUDGE BORK. Not one derived in that [as developed in *Griswold*] fashion. There may be other arguments and I do not want to pass upon those.[32]

Bork's responses to many of the questions led Senator Patrick Leahy and other observers to suggest that he had undergone a "confirmation conversion" in order to gain Senate approval. The "confirmation conversion" language was fueled by documents submitted by Bork's opponents which explicitly compared his confirmation testimony with previous statements on various subjects.[33] One scholar noted later that after several days of testimony Bork had "contradicted much of what he stood for and for which he was nominated."[34]

During their questioning of Bork, several Republican senators, particularly Orrin Hatch and Alan Simpson, accused their colleagues of viciously attacking him and taking his statements out of context. Hatch complained, "Well, what I am concerned about is the way your record is being distorted, some of the inflammatory rhetoric; some of the, I think, unuseful and really false methodology being used."[35] These senators characterized Bork as a mainstream judge and not an extremist, as his opponents were insisting. Simpson argued,

[I]t seems to me so far that the extremism so far in this case and the extremist views and philosophy of Judge Bork, that the extremism is in the rhetoric of the opponents of Judge Bork. That is where it is to this point, and the stridency of that. . . . [W]e have and will have an opportunity to pursue this to find that we have a . . ."conservative judge" who exercises judicial restraint, who tries to leave social policy decisions to the people and their elected representatives where the Constitution does not clearly speak.[36]

At the completion of Bork's testimony, the Judiciary Committee heard additional testimony from a number of witnesses, both in favor of and in opposition to the confirmation. Prepared statements or testimony were provided by distinguished former and current public officials, law professors and other academics, and representatives of several interest groups. The Committee received additional materials for the record from individuals and groups who were not called to testify.[37]

After twelve days of hearings, the Judiciary Committee voted 9–5 to recommend that the full Senate reject the nomination. At that point, Reagan administration officials struggled over whether Bork should request that his name be withdrawn from consideration or press his case to a full Senate vote. Key senators had confirmed publicly that they would vote to reject him, and it was pretty clear that the nomination would be defeated. Nonetheless, Bork opted to let the nomination go to the full Senate for decision. The debate on the floor, which began on October 21, lasted almost three days. On October 23, the Senate voted 58–42 to reject the nomination, the largest margin of defeat of any Supreme Court nominee in history.[38]

The Controversy Continues

Conflict once again ensued in the administration over who the president should select as the next nominee. Both the moderates and conservatives pushed federal appellate judges, Anthony Kennedy and Douglas Ginsburg, respectively. Kennedy, a graduate of Stanford University and Harvard Law School, was serving on the Ninth Circuit Court of Appeals, to which he had been appointed in 1975 by President Gerald Ford. Kennedy was reputed to be a solid conservative, but his record did not manifest the strident conservatism of Robert Bork and other potential candidates. Ginsburg had less experience as a federal judge, having served for only one year on the D.C. Circuit. He received his undergraduate degree from Cornell University and, like Bork, was a graduate of the University of Chicago Law School. Ginsburg had been a professor at Harvard Law School for eight years, and he served in the Justice Department's anti-trust division during the Reagan administration, before being appointed to the federal bench. Ginsburg's background was so similar to Bork's that one scholar later referred to him as "Bork's protégé."[39] Once again the conservatives prevailed, and on October 29 President Reagan announced Ginsburg as his choice. The nomination ran into immediate trouble, however, when problems in his background that had not been discovered by the FBI check arose. Further examination of his background revealed several alleged conflicts of interest during Ginsburg's tenure as a Justice Department official. Most damaging, however, was evidence that he had smoked marijuana with his students when he taught at Harvard Law School. This proved too embarrassing to Reagan administration officials, who advocated strong anti-drug policies, including the "Just Say No" campaign initiated by the president's wife. Consequently, Ginsburg's nomination was withdrawn.

After the Bork and Ginsburg disasters, on November 24 President Reagan recommended Anthony Kennedy as the nominee. Unlike the previous two nominations, Kennedy was confirmed easily, with vocal opposition from only one of the liberal interest groups that actively opposed Bork, the National Organization for Women. While Kennedy was known as a consistent conservative on the federal bench, he did not have a record of conservative writings critical of liberal Warren and Burger Court precedents. In fact, when questioned about constitutional issues Kennedy did not criticize previous decisions that expanded civil rights and liberties in such areas as freedom of expression, privacy, and equal protection. His testimony was markedly different from Bork's, and this influenced the senators who had voted to reject Bork's confirmation. After only three days of hearings, Kennedy was confirmed by a vote of 97–0.[40] In his detailed analysis of the Bork controversy, Ethan Bronner observed: "Few liberals believed that Kennedy's voting record on the high court would please them. He was clearly conservative. But his expansive reading of rights and equality made Bork's opponents feel their fight had been worthwhile."[41]

Although Anthony Kennedy turned out to be a good choice for conservatives, the Bork controversy left them bitter and angry, and they, along with other analysts, accused Bork's opponents of politicizing the Supreme Court appointment process. As noted in the introductory chapter, despite these claims the process always has been political, although perhaps not as obviously confrontational. The perception nonetheless was that the process had been forever altered, and not in a positive way. Determining the accuracy of this perception would have to await future nominations.

CHAPTER TWO

David Souter

A "Home-Run" for Conservatives?

I am most pleased to announce that I will nominate as associate justice of the United States Supreme Court a remarkable judge of keen intellect and the highest ability, one whose scholarly commitment to the law and whose wealth of experience mark him of first rank.[1]

With those words, on July 23, 1990, President George H. W. Bush announced Federal Appeals Court Judge David Souter as his choice to succeed Justice William Brennan on the high court. In a career spanning over three decades, Justice Brennan had established a reputation as the Court's leading liberal and most consistent advocate of civil liberties and civil rights. Souter, a New Hampshire Republican, was reputed to be a conservative, but he was not clearly associated with the conservative movement. Although he initially recommended other candidates for the seat, John Sununu, Bush's conservative chief of staff and former New Hampshire governor, supported the President's choice, and conservatives assumed that Souter would help to solidify a conservative majority on the high court. In fact, Sununu apparently described Souter as a "home-run" for conservatives.[2]

At the time, President Bush's nomination of Souter was viewed by most observers as a clever strategy. By selecting Souter, Bush could appoint a conservative without facing a confirmation battle like the one that followed the nomination of Robert Bork three years earlier. Unlike Bork, Souter did not have a record of controversial writings or speeches that could be used by opponents to block his confirmation. For this reason, commentators and supporters of his nomination began referring to him as a "stealth" candidate. Indeed, President Bush had never even met Souter until he became one of the finalists for the Brennan vacancy.[3]

So who was this unknown, so-called "stealth" candidate? David Souter was born in Melrose, Massachusetts, on September 17, 1939. At the age of eleven, he moved with his parents to Weare, New Hampshire. Souter attended public schools in nearby Concord, and after high school graduation, he enrolled at Harvard College, where he graduated with honors in 1961. After studying at Oxford as a Rhodes Scholar 1961–63, he attended Harvard Law School, receiving his degree in 1966. Souter spent two years in private practice at a firm in Concord and subsequently joined the New Hampshire attorney general's office. After serving for two years as an assistant attorney general, in 1970 he became chief deputy to state Attorney General Warren Rudman. When his term ended, Rudman persuaded the governor to appoint Souter as his successor. Souter served as state attorney general for two years until he was appointed to a judgeship on the state superior court in 1978. Five years later, New Hampshire Governor John Sununu appointed him to the state supreme court, where he served for seven years until President Bush appointed him to the First Circuit Court of Appeals in May of 1990, just three months before nominating him for a seat on the Supreme Court. Ironically, Souter was sworn into office by First Circuit Chief Judge Stephen Breyer, his future colleague on the high court.[4]

Confirmation Politics

Between the time of the nomination in late July and the beginning of the confirmation hearings in mid–September, legal observers, leaders of conservative and liberal interest groups, members of the media, and senators and their staffs speculated about Souter's judicial philosophy and his attitudes about controversial civil rights and liberties issues, including affirmative action, church-state matters, and, of course, abortion. Feminist groups were particularly concerned about whether Souter would provide the fifth vote to overturn *Roe v. Wade*. *Webster v. Reproductive Health Services,*[5] decided a year earlier, had demonstrated that there were four solid votes to overturn *Roe*—Chief Justice Rehnquist and Associate Justices Scalia, White, and Kennedy. Although Justice O'Connor joined the four in upholding a Missouri law that imposed strict regulations on abortion, she would not agree to overturn this longstanding precedent.[6]

Despite some intense and at times heated exchanges, Souter's confirmation hearings were not nearly as rancorous as the Bork proceedings three years earlier. The hearings lasted for only five days, with Souter testifying for two and a half of those days; the remaining time was devoted to testimony from those favoring and opposing confirmation.

One important advantage for Souter was his unequivocally high evaluation by the American Bar Association's Standing Committee on the Federal Judiciary. By a unanimous vote, the committee had rated him "well qualified," the highest evaluation for a Supreme Court nominee. Moreover, Bush advisors carefully coached him in preparation for the hearings.

In his opening statement to the Senate Judiciary Committee, Souter gave a brief chronology of his life, focusing on his childhood in a small town, his undergraduate and post-graduate education in elite institutions, his brief experience as an attorney in private practice, and his work as a government attorney and judge. He emphasized his commitment to public service, which he said began with his pro bono work in private practice. Souter said that this pro bono work, along with his experience as a trial judge, exposed him to people with a variety of life circumstances in various stations of life. He said that as a result of these experiences he had learned two important lessons.

> The first lesson . . . is that whatever court we are in, whatever we are doing, whether we are on a trial court or an appellate court, at the end of our task some human being is going to be affected. Some human life is going to be changed in some way by what we do. . . .
> The second lesson . . . is if, indeed, we are going to be trial judges, whose rulings will affect the lives of other people and who are going to change their lives by what we do, we had better use every power of our minds and our hearts and our beings to get those rulings right.[7]

Souter told the Committee that as a Supreme Court justice he would continue to be influenced by these lessons. In concluding his remarks he said he would join with the other justices to "make the promises of the Constitution a reality for our time, and to preserve the Constitution for the generations that will follow."[8]

For two and a half days, Souter faced intense questioning from senators on both sides of the aisle. While he declined to answer many of the questions with much specificity, senators were impressed by his knowledge of legal and constitutional history and important Supreme Court precedents in a variety of areas. They questioned him about his general judicial philosophy, his approach to precedent, and his views on contemporary constitutional issues and precedents, particularly in the area of civil rights and liberties.

Beyond questions regarding privacy, abortion, civil rights, and other controversial issues, perhaps the most contentious exchanges occurred during questions about some positions that were advocated in legal briefs when Souter served in the New Hampshire attorney general's office in the 1970s. For example, the state opposed as unconstitutional EEOC regulations requiring the state to compile data regarding the racial composition of its workforce. Souter said that the position advocated in the brief was not his personal opinion but that of the state's executive. In addition, he said that constitutional issues being argued were not settled at that point and the state "had a legitimate position which could in good faith be pressed before the courts."[9] He made similar claims with respect to the state's contention that Congress did not have authority to prohibit the use of literacy tests for voting and that lowering the flag over state buildings to commemorate Good Friday did not violate the Establishment Clause.

At the close of his testimony, senators and Court watchers still could not predict how Judge Souter would decide specific cases, but he did succeed in portraying himself as a thoughtful, open-minded jurist. Although he praised Justice Brennan as "one of the most fearlessly principled guardians of the American Constitution that it has ever had and ever will have,"[10] his testimony gave no indication that his judicial performance would be similar to Brennan's. The question for most legal experts and political activists was whether Souter would be a centrist in the mold of retired Justice Lewis Powell or whether he would be more similar to Justice Anthony Kennedy, moderate sounding but clearly conservative. Senators Howard Metzenbaum and Orrin Hatch came to opposite conclusions. Metzenbaum said that Souter could be a Powell but he did not think he would be "a Kennedy nor a Scalia," while Hatch predicted that Souter would be a "centrist in the style of Justice Byron White" who "would evolve in the direction of Scalia and Kennedy."[11]

Ten days after the hearings ended, on September 27, 1990, the Senate Judiciary Committee recommended confirmation by a 13–1 vote, with only Senator Edward Kennedy dissenting. A few days later, Souter was confirmed by the full Senate by a vote of 90–9. Kennedy was joined in dissent by eight other liberal Democrats.

Media Coverage and Interest Group Participation

The print media gave considerable attention to the Souter nomination and confirmation proceedings. From July 24, the day after President Bush announced Souter's nomination, through early August, this story was covered daily by the *New York Times, Washington Post,* and *Wall Street Journal.* Coverage in these major newspapers was sporadic through the rest of August, it picked up again in early September, and it was especially heavy during the period right before the confirmation hearings began until they ended in mid–September. Media attention, however, was not limited to these three major newspapers. A number of significant regional newspapers like the *Boston Globe, Los Angeles Times, St. Louis Post-Dispatch, San Diego Union-Tribune, San Francisco Chronicle,* and *St. Petersburg Times* gave extensive coverage to the nomination. In fact, many of their stories appeared during the second half of August, when coverage by the national papers was more sporadic. Coverage also was given to Souter's nomination by major weekly news magazines, including *Newsweek, U.S. News and World Report, Business Week,* and *The Economist.*[12]

In addition to feature stories, newspapers and news magazines included editorials and op-ed pieces by columnists, law professors, and public officials, including columns written by failed nominee Robert Bork. Many of the stories focused on Souter's experience as New Hampshire attorney general and as a justice on the New Hampshire Supreme Court. Some writers emphasized that Souter's lack of scholarly writings and federal court opinions made it difficult to determine "the real David Souter." A number of pieces speculated about his future performance and long-term impact on the high court. Stories also discussed likely differences between Souter and Justice Brennan's philosophies of constitutional interpretation. Much of the August coverage focused on announcements from various organizations indicating their opposition to or support for confirmation and on predictions about the tenor and outcome of the confirmation hearings. Journalists reported on Souter's pre-confirmation meetings with key senators, and they gave extensive attention to the confirmation proceedings. The *New York Times* provided extended daily excerpts of the hearings.

The broadcast media did not cover the Souter nomination and confirmation very extensively. None of the major television networks (ABC, CBS, NBC) provided live coverage of the hearings. Only PBS (public broadcasting) carried gavel-to-gavel coverage. CNN covered the nomination announcement, and ABC News Nightline did a special feature on the first day of the hearings. Network coverage consisted primarily of brief stories on their evening news shows.[13]

Unlike the Bork nomination, interest group participation was more difficult to predict for Souter. Although he had a long career of public service, first as a government attorney and then as a judge, there was little information by which his views on important issues of the day or his judicial philosophy could be gauged. He had written a number of opinions when he served on the New Hampshire superior court, but they were unpublished. Moreover, as a state supreme court justice, Souter was faced with cases involving zoning disputes, routine criminal appeals, commercial matters, and utility rate increases, not major issues of constitutional law such as those decided by the high court.[14] As *New York Times* reporter Linda Greenhouse noted the day after the nomination was announced, during his two decades of public service, Souter "ha[d] not given a speech, written a law review article or, as far as anyone knows, taken a position on the correctness of Supreme Court precedents on abortion or any other issue."[15] This stood in clear contrast to Bork, who had an extensive record of criticism of *Roe* and other landmark Supreme Court decisions.

As noted in Chapter 1, liberal organizations mounted an all-out offensive against the Bork nomination almost from the moment it was announced. By contrast, while they had concerns about Souter, they disagreed about whether to officially oppose his confirmation. Before the hearings began, the Alliance for Justice and the Leadership Conference on Civil Rights, an umbrella organization that mobilized against the Bork nomination, decided against official opposition.[16] This is not to say, however, that liberal groups remained on the sidelines during the confirmation process. Following Souter's appearance, the Judiciary Committee heard testimony and received statements from a number of prominent liberal organizations, particularly women's rights groups. Representatives of some of these groups urged rejection because Souter had not clearly indicated support for either abortion rights in general or *Roe v. Wade* in particular. Ironically, the Conservative Caucus opposed confirmation because Souter did not commit to overturning *Roe*. Other organizations opposed confirmation based on their concerns about Souter's position on other civil rights and liberties issues.

Groups Testifying Against Confirmation

     National Abortion Rights Action League (NARAL)

     Planned Parenthood

     Mexican-American Legal Defense and Education Fund

     National Council of Jewish Women

     National Organization for Women (NOW)

     NOW Legal Defense and Education Fund

     Fund for the Feminist Majority

     National Lawyers' Guild

     Supreme Court Watch

     Lambda Legal Defense and Education Fund

     National Gay and Lesbian Task Force

     Center for Constitutional Rights

     The Conservative Caucus, Inc.

Senators also heard testimony from representatives of organizations in favor of the nomination, particularly the ABA Standing Committee on the Federal Judiciary and law enforcement associations. Also, the Hispanic National Bar Association expressed some reservations but nonetheless recommended confirmation.

Groups Testifying in Favor of Confirmation

     American Bar Association Standing Committee on the Federal Judiciary

     New Hampshire Bar Association

     Hispanic National Bar Association

     Mothers Against Drunk Driving (MADD)

     International Association of Chiefs of Police

National Sheriffs Association

National Troopers Coalition

Fraternal Order of Police

Several additional groups testified but did not urge either confirmation or rejection. The National Association of Women Judges and California Women Lawyers urged senators to study Souter's record carefully, and the latter requested that they pay special attention to women's issues. The Leadership Conference on Civil Rights expressed serious concerns about the nomination, and, while some individual groups in this umbrella organization urged rejection, the entire organization did not take this position at the hearings. The Southeastern Legal Foundation commented on the advise and consent role of the Senate in Supreme Court confirmations, asserting that it was inappropriate for organizations to raise questions about nominees' opinions on particular issues because they would be introducing a "political agenda" to the process.

Several other organizations that were not called to testify nevertheless provided written statements for the record. These included the Alliance for Justice, Coalition for America, Citizens for God and Country, International Narcotics Enforcement Officers Association, National Association of Criminal Defense Lawyers, National Women's Law Center, Society of American Law Teachers, and the Women's Legal Defense Fund.

After the hearings ended, the Leadership Conference on Civil Rights and the Alliance for Justice reversed course, deciding to urge Senators to vote against confirmation. The National Association for the Advancement of Colored People (NAACP), the oldest black civil rights organization, also publicly opposed confirmation. On the other hand, the ACLU and People for the American Way did not concur with these two groups.

Judicial Performance

Not surprisingly, scholars and other legal observers have focused a great deal of attention on Souter's performance on the Supreme Court. An analysis of his record thus far illustrates a remarkable evolution from a conservative justice in his early tenure to one who is more likely to be aligned with his more liberal colleagues. In this sense, Souter's record is similar to that of Justice Harry Blackmun, who began his career on the Supreme Court as a conservative but gradually evolved to become the most liberal member on the Court at the time he retired in 1993. This section will focus on Souter's voting behavior and written opinions. Particular attention will be paid to cases involving issues that were prominently discussed during his confirmation hearings.

The First Term: 1990–1991

Was David Souter the "stealth" nominee that conservatives hoped for and liberals dreaded? Based solely on his early tenure on the Court, especially his first term, the answer appeared to be yes. He had a conservative voting record, and he was aligned with the Court's conservative wing in the most closely-watched cases of the term.

During the 1990–1991 term, Justice Souter voted consistently with the conservative members of the Court. According to one study, in the 65 nonunanimous cases, Souter was a member of a voting bloc composed of conservative justices—Rehnquist, Scalia, Kennedy, O'Connor, and White.[17] He was characterized as a moderate conservative, however, because he voted most frequently with Justice O'Connor rather than with Justices Scalia and Rehnquist, the most conservative justices. Another study of cases involving civil rights and liberties issues showed that Souter voted for a liberal outcome in only 35% of the cases and that he was aligned with a conservative voting bloc that included Chief Justice Rehnquist and Justices O'Connor and Kennedy. His voting behavior stood in marked contrast to that of his predecessor, William Brennan, who had an 86% liberal voting record in his final four terms on the Court.[18] Moreover, Souter provided the fifth vote for conservative outcomes in seven criminal justice decisions that likely would have been decided differently with Brennan on the Court.[19]

Despite his conservative voting record, however, it was difficult to determine with any degree of specificity Souter's views on various issues during his first term because he wrote so few opinions. He authored only 12 opinions—eight majority, two concurrences, and two dissents. Chief Justice Rehnquist wrote the next fewest—21—but 15 of those were majority opinions. Souter's majority opinion total is consistent with one aspect of the "freshman effect" phenomenon, which indicates that new justices receive fewer majority opinion assignments than their senior colleagues because the newcomers have not been fully integrated or socialized into their roles on the Court. In this respect, Souter was similar to other recent appointees—Justices Kennedy, Scalia, and O'Connor.[20] In addition, he did not write the majority opinion in any of the "important" cases as determined by recognition in the *New York Times* and *Congressional Quarterly* summaries of the term. Despite being given few majority opinion assignments, new justices often utilize concurrences and dissents to assert their viewpoints on various issues, but Souter refrained from doing so.[21]

Souter's majority opinions came primarily in decisions where the vote was unanimous or in cases that involved narrow, technical legal matters rather than controversial issues or subjects of broader scope and applicability.[22] He did write a concurring opinion in an important criminal justice case. In *Payne v. Tennessee* (1991), Souter joined a six-person majority to overrule two precedents that had prohibited the use of so-called victim impact statements at sentencing hearings in capital cases.[23] The two earlier cases had held that such statements could result in capricious application of the death penalty because focus would be placed on the value of the victim's life rather than on the severity of the defendant's crime. Souter's concurrence contended that it was perfectly appropriate to consider victim impact statements in capital sentencing decisions. In his view, rather than leading to arbitrary sentencing for the defendant, excluding victim impact statements likely would result in excessive leniency.

In perhaps the most closely watched First Amendment case of the term, Souter endorsed a very conservative decision. In *Rust v. Sullivan* (1991), he was part of a five-member majority that upheld the "gag rule," a federal regulation prohibiting clinics that receive federal funds from counseling patients about abortion.[24] Justice Blackmun's dissent characterized the gag rule as impermissibly intruding on the doctor/patient dialogue and restricting information about abortion from women who rely solely on federally funded clinics for their health care. Souter's endorsement of the majority opinion is somewhat perplexing, given his testimony to the Judiciary Committee. As a trustee of a New Hampshire community hospital in the 1970s, Souter had supported a change in policy that permitted the hospital to begin to perform abortions. At confirmation, he had said that the hospital had an obligation to provide community members seeking an abortion "the greatest degree of safety in medical care," given its nonsectarian nature.[25] It seems odd, then, that he would support a policy which restricts patients from even receiving information about abortion.

Souter took positions in two other First Amendment cases that reflect a more moderate approach than that of the conservative majority. In *Barnes v. Glen Theatre, Inc.* (1991), by a 5–4 vote, the Court ruled that states may prohibit nude dancing in bars because the state's interest in promoting public order and morality was greater than the dancers' interest in freedom of expression.[26] Souter concurred in the judgment only, emphasizing his view that the state's regulation was justified not by its desire to promote public morality, but by its interest in protecting the public from harms associated with nude dancing in adult entertainment establishments, including prostitution, sexual assault, and other crimes. The Court held in *Cohen v. Cowles Media Co.* (1991) that the First Amendment did not preclude a newspaper from being sued when it broke a promise of confidentiality given to a news source. Justice White's majority opinion concluded that the media are not excluded from the reach of generally applicable laws even if their enforcement makes it difficult to gather and report the news. Joined in dissent by Justices Marshall, Blackmun, and O'Connor, Souter argued that the press should be protected in order to provide important information to the public. He concluded that "the State's interest in enforcing a newspaper's promise of confidentiality [was] insufficient to outweigh the interest in unfettered publication of the information revealed in this case."[27]

Evolution of a Judicial Moderate/Liberal

His first term notwithstanding, Souter has disappointed conservative supporters who expected him to become a reliable conservative voice on the high court. In his second and third terms, 1991–1992 and 1992–1993, he began to shift away from the conservative wing. For example, in civil rights and liberties cases his percentage of liberal voting increased from 35% in his first term to 54% and 57% in his second and third terms, respectively, and he was not a member of any voting blocs.[28] In fact, at the end of his third term, Thomas Jipping of the Free Congress Foundation quipped, "John Sununu told me directly that Souter would be a 'home-run' for conservatives. . . . The first term, I thought he might be a blooper single. After last year, I thought he was a foul ball. Now I think he's a strikeout."[29]

Souter's movement away from the conservative wing of the Court has continued in subsequent terms. According to *Harvard Law Review's* end-of-term statistics, for all cases decided with written opinions in the 1995–1996 through 1998–1999 terms, he had the highest agreement with Justices Ginsburg (83%) and Breyer (82%). In the 1999–2000 term, Souter agreed most often with Justice Ginsburg (88%), Justice Breyer (82%), and, for the first time, Justice Stevens (84%), the strongest liberal currently on the Court.[30] As Joan Biskupic of the *Washington Post* pointed out at the end of the 1998–1999 term, however, using the term liberal to describe Justices Stevens, Souter, Ginsburg, and Breyer is somewhat of a misnomer. She noted that although the four "stand to the left of the potent [conservative] majority bloc, they do not stand for the judicial liberalism as it was known even a decade ago, when the justices trying to block the newly consolidated Rehnquist majority were Justices William J. Brennan, Jr., Harry A. Blackmun, Thurgood Marshall, and Stevens—then the most conservative of the four."[31]

Focusing on voting data on all the cases in a term provides some insight into the dynamics on the Court, but examining voting behavior in nonunanimous cases provides a more complete picture of voting patterns. Beginning with the 1997–1998 term, the Harvard statistical summary includes voting alignments for nonunanimous cases, and Souter's scores with the other "liberal" justices are similar to those from all the cases. In 1997–1998 and 1998–1999, he had the highest agreement with Justices Ginsburg (66% and 77%) and Breyer (64% and 70%). He had only moderate levels of agreement with Justice Stevens in those two terms (45% and 54%). In the 1999–2000 term, however, his agreement score with Justice Stevens jumped dramatically to 76%, and he again had high levels of agreement with Justices Ginsburg (82%) and Breyer (72%). By contrast, he agreed with Justices Thomas and Scalia only 30% of the time in nonunanimous cases in the 1997–1998 and 1998–1999 terms, and his agreement with Justices O'Connor, Rehnquist, and Kennedy was in the middle 40% range. By the 1999–2000 term,

Souter was in agreement with Justice Scalia in less than 20% of the nonunanimous cases, and his agreement with the remaining justices ranged from 30% to 44%.

Abortion

Souter's decision in *Rust v. Sullivan* from his first term encouraged both conservatives and liberals to think that in the future he might indeed provide a fifth vote to overturn *Roe* and leave abortion policy up to the states. At confirmation, despite continual prodding, Souter steadfastly refused to state his beliefs about abortion. In response to a question by Senator Howard Metzenbaum about the difficulty faced by women with unwanted pregnancies, particularly as a result of rape, incest, failed contraceptives, or inadequate health information, Souter told a story from his law school days at Harvard. As an adviser for freshman students, he counseled the girlfriend of one of his advisees who was pregnant and contemplating a self-induced abortion. He gave a clever and thoughtful response which showed sensitivity toward the issue of abortion without indicating how he would rule on *Roe*.

> I know you will respect the privacy of the people involved, and I will not try to say what I told her. But I spent 2 hours in a small dormitory bedroom that afternoon, in that room because that was the most private place we could get so that no one in the next suite of rooms could hear, listening to her and trying to counsel her to approach her problem in a way different from what she was doing, and your question has brought that back to me.
>
> I think the only thing I can add to that is I know what you were trying to tell me, because I remember that afternoon.[32]

On the final day of the 1991–1992 term, in a case involving a very restrictive Pennsylvania statute, the nation finally learned where Souter stood with respect to *Roe*. In *Planned Parenthood v. Casey* (1992), the justices heard a challenge to Pennsylvania's comprehensive abortion regulations, which called for informed consent procedures, a twenty-four-hour waiting period, parental consent for minors, spousal notification, and public reporting and disclosure requirements.[33] These provisions were nearly identical to earlier ones that had been struck down by the Court in *Akron v. Akron Center for Reproductive Health* (1983) and *Thornburgh v. American College of Obstetricians and Gynecologists* (1986).

The decision in *Casey* was a fragmented one with no majority opinion. One group—consisting of Chief Justice Rehnquist and Justices Scalia, White, and Thomas—voted to uphold all of the challenged provisions and called for *Roe* to be explicitly overruled. Justice Blackmun, however, voted to strike all of the provisions, and Justice Stevens rejected all but the informed consent and reporting requirements. A joint opinion by a trio consisting of Justices Souter, O'Connor, and Kennedy controlled the outcome of this case. They voted to uphold all of the provisions except for the spousal notification requirement, but held that "the essential holding of *Roe v. Wade* should be retained and once again reaffirmed."[34] The trio emphasized a concern for the principle of stare decisis and for preserving the integrity and legitimacy of the Court. "A decision to overrule *Roe*'s essential holding under the existing circumstances would address error, if error there was, at the cost of both profound and unnecessary damage to the Court's legitimacy, and to the Nation's commitment to the rule of law."[35] This section of the opinion focusing on the appropriateness of overruling precedent was written primarily by Souter. Despite the trio's claims that the "central holding" of *Roe* was reaffirmed, their opinion substantially modified that ruling. Specifically, *Roe*'s trimester framework was abandoned and was replaced with a test advocated by Justice O'Connor in earlier cases. Under this new approach, an abortion regulation is invalid if it places an "undue burden" on a woman's abortion decision. A regulation poses an undue burden "if its purpose or effect is to place a substantial obstacle in the path of a woman seeking an abortion before the fetus attains viability."

In the years following *Casey*, abortion opponents continued to introduce regulations to impede women's access to abortions. One type of restriction, so-called "partial birth abortion" laws, have been passed by a number of states. In *Stenberg v. Carhart* (2000), Souter joined the majority in striking down a Nebraska partial birth abortion statute, ruling that the law posed an undue burden on a woman's right to abortion.[36]

Church-State Issues

In cases involving the Establishment Clause, Souter consistently has rejected government accommodation, an approach favored by conservatives that generally permits substantial government involvement with religion. In *Lee v. Weisman* (1992), decided in Souter's second term, the justices ruled on the constitutionality of government-sponsored prayers at public school graduation ceremonies.[37] An amicus brief filed by the Bush Justice Department urged the Court to use this case to abandon the *Lemon* test, a doctrine that supports government neutrality, and to adopt the accommodationist approach. Justice Kennedy's majority opinion did not overrule *Lemon,* holding the prayers unconstitutional based on earlier decisions regarding government-sponsored religious activities in public schools. Souter joined Kennedy's opinion and added a concurrence advocating government neutrality as the proper approach to church-state issues.

> While the Establishment Clause's concept of neutrality is not self-revealing, our recent cases have invested it with specific content: the state may not favor or endorse either religion generally over nonreligion or one religion over others. This principle against favoritism and endorsement has become the foundation of Establishment Clause jurisprudence, ensuring that religious belief is irrelevant to every citizen's standing in the

political community, and protecting religion from the demeaning effects of any governmental embrace. Now, as in the early Republic, "religion & Govt. will both exist in greater purity, the less they are mixed together."[38]

Souter's belief that the Establishment Clause prohibits government involvement with religion is seen in his votes and opinions in several other cases. He sharply criticized the majority opinion in *Rosenberger v. University of Virginia* (1995), which decided that public universities may provide funding to student groups for religious publications without violating the Establishment Clause. He wrote that "using public funds for the direct subsidization of preaching the word is categorically forbidden under the Establishment Clause, and if the Clause was meant to accomplish nothing else, it was meant to bar this use of public money."[39] In later cases Souter voted against programs involving parochial aid (government funding to private religious schools) in *Agostini v. Felton* (1997) and *Mitchell v. Helms* (2000), writing strong dissents in both cases.[40] He insisted that the programs in these cases amounted to direct religious subsidies by the government, something forbidden by the Establishment Clause. Souter also joined a six-member majority in *Santa Fe Independent School District v. Doe* (2000) to strike down school-sponsored, student-led prayers at public high school football games.[41]

Civil Rights

Souter's views on civil rights issues were at the heart of the confirmation hearings. He was subjected to a barrage of questions about the standards for deciding Fourteenth Amendment equal protection cases, affirmative action, and recent Supreme Court cases involving employment discrimination. Antonia Hernandez, president and general counsel of the Mexican-American Legal Defense and Education Fund, told the Judiciary Committee that "Judge Souter ha[d] not demonstrated fairness or even compassion for racial minorities, particularly with regard to our trying to win nondiscriminatory opportunities to equal employment, and to our most fundamental right under the Constitution and the laws of our country, the right to vote."[42] In his statement before the Committee, Joseph Rauh, general counsel for the Leadership Conference on Civil Rights, asserted that Souter was insensitive to racial problems.

Souter's performance on civil rights issues, particularly gender discrimination, must be surprising to the liberal groups which expressed serious doubts about—and in some cases opposition to—his confirmation. For example, he voted to invalidate Virginia Military Institute's (VMI) exclusively male admission policy as unconstitutional gender discrimination in *U.S. v. Virginia* (1996) and to apply the Equal Protection Clause to claims of sexual orientation in *Romer v. Evans* (1996). He did not write separate opinions in either of these cases, but his endorsement of Justice Ginsburg's opinion in the VMI case is interesting in light of his confirmation testimony. Justice Ginsburg's use of the phrases "skeptical scrutiny" and "exceedingly persuasive justification" led Justice Scalia to accuse the majority of incorrectly applying the intermediate standard and of redefining it to make it indistinguishable from strict scrutiny, the highest level of review. As New Hampshire attorney general, in 1978 Souter wrote a brief challenging the Court's adoption of intermediate- or middle-level scrutiny as the standard for equal protection claims involving gender discrimination. Under this standard, gender classifications can be upheld only if they are substantially related to the achievement of important government objectives. When questioned about this and whether he believed the Court should return to minimal scrutiny for these types of cases, Souter said that his position in 1978 was as an advocate, and perhaps there actually should be a higher level of scrutiny for gender discrimination cases. He viewed the current middle-level standard as not protective enough because it is "too loose" and leaves too much discretion to reviewing courts. "[T]he question . . . is whether there can be devised a middle-tier test providing a higher level of scrutiny for . . . classifications on the basis of sex and illegitimacy that does not suffer from the capacity of a court, as a practical matter, to read it back down to the lowest level of scrutiny."[43]

Souter also has taken a liberal position in sexual harassment cases, an issue of great concern to the women's rights groups who opposed his confirmation. For example, he wrote the majority opinion in *Faragher v. Boca Raton* (1998), in which the Court ruled that employers could be held liable for conduct of a supervisor that creates a hostile work environment. They could avoid liability, however, if they could demonstrate that (1) they "exercised reasonable care to prevent and correct promptly any sexually harassing behavior" and (2) the employee "unreasonably failed to take advantage of any preventive or corrective opportunities provided by the employer."[44] In a companion case, *Burlington Industries, Inc. v. Ellerth* (1998), Souter also joined the majority's holding that employers could be held liable in a "quid-pro-quo" sexual harassment case even if the employee did not suffer any tangible, adverse job consequences.[45] By contrast, Justices Thomas and Scalia concluded that employers should be liable in such situations only if the employee could prove that the employer was negligent in allowing the supervisor's conduct to occur. Also in 1998, in *Gebser v. Lago Vista Independent School District,* Souter dissented from the ruling that school districts cannot be held financially liable for a teacher's harassment of a student unless the student has informed a school official who has reasonable authority to take action to remedy the problem.[46]

While the high court has upheld a number of affirmative action programs,[47] by the time that Souter was nominated, the Court's support for affirmative action was dwindling. In 1989, in *City of Richmond v. Croson,* by a 6–3 vote the Court struck down a set-aside program for government contracting that was patterned after an earlier federal program that had been upheld in 1980.[48] In *Croson* the majority held that the 1980 *Fullilove* precedent was not applicable because, under the Fourteenth Amendment, Congress has more latitude in remedying discrimination than do state and local governments. This decision led a number of Court observers to speculate that the Court was unlikely to uphold affirmative action programs in the future. One year later, however, by a slim 5–4 vote, the justices upheld a federal program designed to assist the Federal Communications Commission in promoting broadcast diversity.[49] Justice Brennan's majority opinion in *Metro Broadcasting v. FCC* (1990) used language from *Croson* regarding the distinction between federal authority and state and local power to remedy discrimination.

Given Justice Brennan's support for affirmative action programs, and especially his role in *Metro Broadcasting,* there was intense interest in Souter's views on this subject during the confirmation hearings. He expressed general support for affirmative action but was unclear about whether he supported the ruling in *Metro Broadcasting.* "I would suppose it would go without saying today that if we are . . . to have the kind of society which I described yesterday as the society which I knew or found reflected in my home, there will be a need—and I am afraid for a longer time than we would like to say—a need for affirmative action which seeks out qualified people who have been discouraged by generations of societal discrimination from taking their place in the mainstream."[50] On the question of whether affirmative action remedies must be limited to individuals who can prove specific acts of discrimination, Souter was less concrete. "[T]here are going to be some cases in which the only thing that is going to be proven is . . . a specific act of discrimination. There are going to be other cases . . . in [which] what is proven is, in fact, a far broader but proven discrimination. And the remedy must be tailored to the proof."[51]

His general support for affirmative action is reflected in his dissenting opinion in the only substantive affirmative action case decided since his appointment to the Court. In *Adarand Constructors, Inc. v. Pena* (1995), the high court overturned its 1990 *Metro Broadcasting* decision, ruling that all government affirmative action programs—federal, state, and local—would be decided using strict scrutiny. In her majority opinion, Justice O'Connor insisted that this did not mean the end of government-sponsored affirmative action. "The unhappy persistence of both the practice and the lingering effects of racial discrimination against minority groups in this country is an unfortunate reality, and government is not disqualified from acting in response to it."[52] The Court did not invalidate the program challenged here but remanded the case to the lower court for reconsideration using strict scrutiny.

Souter dissented, arguing that the Court should not have addressed the issue of which standard to apply because *Fullilove* was sufficient to decide the case. In

Fullilove, the Court upheld a federal set-aside program in government contracting because the government had provided evidence that persistent discrimination in the construction industry decreased opportunities for minority contractors. Souter concluded that the statutes at issue in *Adarand* were better tailored than the one upheld in *Fullilove,* and he endorsed the use of affirmative action to remedy discrimination. "Constitutional authority to remedy past discrimination is not limited to the power to forbid its continuation, but extends to eliminating those effects that would otherwise persist and skew the operation of public systems even in the absence of current intent to practice any discrimination."[53] He conceded that the type of program at issue here may harm "innocent" whites who are not personally responsible for the discrimination, but he said that the temporary nature of the program and its attempt to eliminate the lingering effects of discrimination justify this result.

Redistricting plans that result in the creation of so-called majority-minority legislative districts is another civil rights issue that has divided liberals and conservatives, both on the Court and in the larger society. Conservatives contend that these plans improperly consider race, while liberals maintain that they are necessary to remedy past and present discrimination against minorities in the electoral process. This, too, is an area where Souter has disappointed the conservatives who supported his nomination. Beginning with *Shaw v. Reno* in 1993, Souter has criticized the majority for adopting strict scrutiny as the standard for examining such redistricting plans, which have been challenged as violations of the Equal Protection Clause. He maintained in *Shaw* that the Court had always "analyzed equal protection claims involving race in electoral districting different from equal protection claims involving other forms of governmental conduct."[54] Three years later, when the Court used strict scrutiny to invalidate four majority-minority congressional districts in North Carolina and Texas—*Shaw v. Hunt* (1996) and *Bush v. Vera* (1996)—Souter issued a strong dissent, asserting "it is impossible . . . to apply 'traditional districting principles' in areas with substantial minority populations without considering race."[55] In 2001, Souter voted with the majority to uphold the North Carolina district that had been reconfigured by the state after it was struck down in *Hunt.*

Federalism

In recent years, federalism has returned to the Court's agenda as an important issue, as some public officials at both the state and federal levels have contended that the federal government has improperly usurped state authority in a number of areas. During the hearings, Souter discussed the problems of federalism as a political problem stemming from states' unwillingness to use their powers to address problems that the people wished to have addressed. The result was that the people began to look toward the federal government to resolve these problems. States' rights advocates have cited the Tenth Amendment's provision that "powers not delegated to the United States by the Constitution, nor prohibited by it to the States, are reserved to the states" as support for limiting federal authority. Responding to Senator Strom Thurmond's question about this amendment, Souter said, "any approach to the Tenth amendment today is an approach which has got to take into consideration constitutional developments outside of the Tenth amendment [such as the growth of the commerce power and federal authority under the Fourteenth Amendment] which . . . would have astonished the Framers."[56]

Before Souter's appointment, the Court's most recent major federalism case was *Garcia v. San Antonio Metropolitan Transit Authority* (1985), which upheld the application of the Fair Labor Standards Act's (FLSA) minimum wage and maximum hour provisions to state public employees over objections that this violated state sovereignty.[57] *Garcia* overturned the earlier ruling from *National League of Cities v. Usery* (1976), holding that Congress's extension of the FLSA provisions to state employees unconstitutionally infringed on the sovereignty of the states.[58] Federalism issues returned to the Court in *New York v. United States* (1992), where the justices were faced with a challenge to three provisions of the Low-Level Radioactive Waste Policy Amendments Act of 1985.[59] By a 6–3 vote, the Court upheld two of the provisions as consistent with the Tenth Amendment but struck down the third as exceeding Congress's enumerated powers, thereby unconstitutionally infringing state sovereignty. Souter joined Justice O'Connor's majority opinion, which contained strong language endorsing state authority. In the concluding paragraphs she wrote, "The Constitution . . . 'leaves to the several States a residuary and inviolable sovereignty' reserved explicitly to the States by the Tenth Amendment. Whatever the outer limits of that sovereignty may be, one thing is clear: The Federal Government may not compel the States to enact or administer a federal regulatory program."[60]

By contrast, in cases decided since then, Souter has adopted positions that support the extensive exercise of federal power. In *Printz v. United States* (1997), a five-member majority invalidated a provision of the federal Brady Handgun Violence Prevention Act of 1993 requiring local law enforcement officers to conduct background checks on gun buyers until a national database for instant background checks was in operation.[61] The majority, emphasizing that the structure of the Constitution is based on dual sovereignty of the federal and state governments, said that the federal government was not authorized to compel state or local officials to carry out federal programs. While joining Justice Stevens's broader dissenting opinion, Souter wrote a brief separate dissent arguing that Alexander Hamilton's statements in Federalist No. 27 show that the federal government, "when exercising an otherwise legitimate power," is authorized to "require state 'auxiliaries' to take appropriate action."[62]

Although the *Printz* decision did not invalidate the entire Brady Bill, some commentators viewed it as a signal that the Court might be returning to its pre-*Garcia* position of limiting federal authority in favor of state sovereignty. Two years later, the decision in *Alden v. Maine* (1999) fueled further speculation about the direction of the Court's federalism jurisprudence.[63] In *Alden,* a five-member majority held that state employees cannot bring suits in state courts seeking enforcement of the Fair Labor Standards Act (FLSA). The suit was brought by a group of probation officers in Maine, whose previous suit in federal court had been dismissed as the result of an earlier decision in *Seminole Tribe of Fla. v. Florida* (1996), which concluded that the Eleventh Amendment provides states with sovereign immunity from suits in federal courts. In *Alden,* based on its analysis of the Tenth Amendment and the history and structure of the Constitution, the majority extended this immunity to suits in state courts seeking enforcement of federal rights. In a lengthy and pointed dissent, Souter argued that the majority's analysis was plainly in error. "The Court's federalism ignores the accepted authority of Congress to bind States under the FLSA and to provide for enforcement of federal rights in state court. The Court's history simply disparages the capacity of the Constitution to order relationships in a Republic that has changed since the founding."[64]

In 2000 and 2001, Souter dissented from two additional decisions limiting federal authority: *Kimel v. Florida Board of Regents* and *Board of Trustees of the University of Alabama v. Garrett.*[65] In *Kimel,* the Court held that states are immune from suits under the federal Age Discrimination in Employment Act. *Garrett* ruled that state employees may not sue their states for violations of the federal Americans with Disabilities Act.

Commerce Powers

Beginning in 1937, the Supreme Court adopted an expansive interpretation of Congress's commerce powers, utilizing a broad definition of interstate commerce that permitted federal regulation of a variety of economic activities. Between 1937 and 1995, only once did the Court rule that a federal regulation under the Commerce Clause was beyond congressional authority. In 1976 the Court held that the minimum wage and maximum hour provisions of the Fair Labor Standards Act could not be applied to state and local governments, but nine years later the Court reversed this decision.[66]

After years of being dormant, the scope of congressional power under the Commerce Clause returned as an important issue to the Court in the 1994–1995 term. In *United States v. Lopez* (1995), a narrow majority struck down the Gun Free School Zones Act of 1990 as in improper exercise of congressional commerce power.[67] After reviewing the major historical and modern precedents on the federal commerce power, Chief Justice Rehnquist's majority opinion held that the appropriate test requires the Court to determine whether the activity being regulated "substantially affects" interstate commerce. He applied that test to the Gun Free School Zones Act and concluded that there was no substantial effect on interstate commerce over the government's claims that firearm possession in a school zone could lead to violent crime, which could in turn affect the national economy. Souter joined Justice Breyer's dissent, which accepted the government's claims about the relationship between guns in schools and interstate commerce as legitimate. In addition, he wrote separately to express concern that the majority had not acted with restraint and did not properly defer to congressional judgments regarding the Commerce Clause as required by modern precedents.

> The modern respect for the competence and primacy of Congress in matters affecting commerce developed only after one of this Court's most chastening experiences, when it perforce repudiated an earlier and untenably expansive conception of judicial review in derogation of congressional commerce power. . . .[T]oday's decision tugs the Court off course, leading it to suggest opportunities for further developments that would be at odds with the rule of restraint to which the Court still wisely states adherence.[68]

Souter dissented from a decision in 2000 that struck down a portion of the Violence Against Women Act (VAWA) as a violation of federal commerce power. The majority concluded that gender-motivated violence did not "substantially affect" interstate commerce and therefore was beyond congressional authority to regulate. Souter chided the majority for disputing what he said was "the mountain of data assembled by Congress . . . showing the effects of violence against women on interstate commerce."[69]

General Judicial Philosophy

Justice Souter does not appear to have an overarching philosophy that consistently shapes his decision making. Instead, he seems to be a pragmatist who is concerned with the context of cases and with case outcomes and their impact. This is not surprising, given his confirmation statements characterizing controversial Supreme Court decisions as practical or pragmatic and his concern about making the "right" decisions because those decisions affect people's lives.

When he was nominated, many speculated that he might adhere to the doctrine of original intent for constitutional interpretation, an approach espoused by many conservatives, including failed nominee Robert Bork. Souter described his own approach in a question from Senator Dennis DeConcini of Arizona regarding his interpretation of the Equal Protection Clause.

> SENATOR DECONCINI. Original intent, then, in what you are telling me is not applicable to your interpretation of the equal protection clause in the Fourteenth Amendment?

JUDGE SOUTER. That is exactly right. I do not believe that the appropriate criterion of constitutional meaning is this sense of specific intent, that you may never apply a provision to any subject except the subject specifically intended by the people who adopted it.

The reason *Brown* [*v. Board of Education*] was correctly decided is not because [the Fourteenth Amendment's Framers and adopters] intended to apply the equal protection clause to school desegregation, but because they did not confine the equal protection clause to those specific or a specifically enumerated list of applications, the equal protection clause is, by its very terms, a clause of general application.

What we are looking for, then, when we look to its original meaning is the principle that was intended to be applied, and if that principle is broad enough to apply to school desegregation, as it clearly was, then that was an appropriate application for it and *Brown* was undoubtedly correctly applied.[70]

Souter reaffirmed this theme in a later exchange with Senator Joseph Biden.

THE CHAIRMAN. You have explained that your approach is to start with the text of the constitutional provision in question; and then if the text is unclear, the judge should proceed to examine not the original intent, but the original meaning.

JUDGE SOUTER. That is correct.

THE CHAIRMAN. Is that correct?

JUDGE SOUTER. Yes, and I mentioned that when I speak of original intent, or the intentionalist school, I am talking particularly about that view that the meaning of the provision or the application of the provision should somehow be confined to those specific instances or problems which were in the minds of those who adopted and ratified the provision, and that the provision should be applied only to those instances or problems. I do not accept that view.[71]

Language from his dissent in *Alden* reflects what he said in his testimony. Responding to the majority's contention that having states subjected to federal suits in their courts would have surprised the Framers, Souter declared, "The Framers' intentions and expectations count so far as they point to the meaning of the Constitution's text or the fair implications of its structure, but they do not hover over the instrument to veto any application of its principles to a world that the Framers could not have anticipated."[72]

When senators asked about his approach to statutory interpretation, Souter expressed a similar view. In contrast to Justice Scalia and others who maintain that a statute should be interpreted solely by examining its text without regard to legislative history, Souter said that, in situations where the text is unclear, courts must use "reliable legislative history." He affirmed this approach early in his tenure on the Court. In a 1992 case involving a section of the National Firearms Act, Justice Scalia sharply criticized Souter's plurality opinion for its use of legislative history. Souter responded in a footnote.

Justice Scalia upbraids us for reliance on legislative history, his "St. Jude of the hagiology of statutory construction." The shrine, however, is well peopled (though it has room for one more), and its congregation has included such noted elders as Justice Frankfurter: "A statute, like other living organisms, derives significance and sustenance from its environment, from which it cannot be severed without being mutilated. Especially is this true where the statute . . . is part of a legislative process having a history and a purpose. The meaning of such a statute cannot be gained by confining inquiry within its four corners. Only the historic process of which such legislation is an incomplete fragment—that to which it gave rise as well as that which gave rise to it—can yield its true meaning."[73]

Summary

Souter portrayed himself to the Senate Judiciary Committee as a judicial moderate, and that is a reasonably accurate description of his performance so far. During his first term (1990–1991), however, it appeared that he might indeed be the "stealth" nominee that so many had predicted. During that term, he was aligned with the Court's conservative wing, and his votes helped to produce conservative rulings that would have been decided differently were his predecessor still on the Court. By his third term, however, Souter was emerging as a moderate voice, much to the dismay of conservatives who had supported his nomination. In more recent terms, Souter has moved even farther away from the conservative wing. This has been especially true in First Amendment, civil rights, and federalism cases, and he has become increasingly liberal in criminal justice cases as well.[74] Occasionally, however, Souter takes positions that baffle even the most astute Court observers. For example, in *Atwater v. City of Lago Vista*, a closely watched Fourth Amendment case from the 2000–2001 term, Souter joined with the conservatives and wrote the majority opinion that permits police officers to conduct full custodial arrests for minor criminal offenses, including those punishable only by fine.[75] Gail Atwater had been arrested for violating Texas's seatbelt restraint law. She then was handcuffed, taken to the local police station, and jailed for about an hour. Rejecting her claim that her right against unreasonable search and seizure was violated, Souter conceded that her arrest and booking were "inconvenient and embarrassing" but concluded that no Fourth Amendment violation occurred. By contrast, the dissenters warned that the majority's decision provides police officers with significant discretion to make arrests for misdemeanor violations and that this discretion "carries with it grave potential for abuse."[76]

During his tenure on the Supreme Court, Souter has evolved from a member of the conservative majority to a moderate-to-liberal justice who often finds himself in the minority. Some have attributed this shift to his close relationship with Justice Brennan, with whom he developed a close personal and professional relationship after Brennan retired.[77] Others have suggested that Souter was misread from the beginning. Thomas Rath, a close friend who served as Souter's deputy attorney general in New Hampshire, explained it this way: "People tried to make him into something he was not. They mistook a person who is conservative politically for one who would be a conservative activist on the bench."[78]

CHAPTER THREE

Clarence Thomas

Dependable Conservative

On July 1, 1991, Justice Thurgood Marshall announced that he was stepping down after twenty-four years of service on the high court. Despite the fact that he had suffered from serious health problems over the years, which often had led to speculation about his retirement, Marshall had vowed to remain on the Court until his death. Thus his announcement took some Court experts by surprise. To others, however, his retirement was not surprising. During his latter years, Marshall reportedly had become frustrated about the Court's conservative decisions on affirmative action, the death penalty, and other important civil rights issues. Moreover, the previous year, he had lost his ideological soulmate on the Court when Justice William Brennan, his longtime liberal ally, retired.

As noted in previous chapters, Supreme Court vacancies always generate intense interest, and this was even more true with Marshall's retirement. He had earned a reputation as a fierce advocate of civil rights and racial equality, first as the leading litigator for the NAACP Legal Defense and Educational Fund, then as a Supreme Court justice. Given Marshall's record, many members of the civil rights community called for President George H.W. Bush to appoint another African American with a strong record of advocacy for civil rights and racial justice. At the same time, the President's more conservative supporters insisted that the nomination of a strong conservative justice would help move the Court in a more conservative direction. Bush ultimately chose Clarence Thomas, an African American, but one with very strong conservative credentials.

Some analysts viewed the nomination as an astute political move. Because some white liberal Democratic senators relied on significant black constituencies for reelection, it could be difficult for them to oppose confirmation of an African American judge. As the authors of one study noted, "If Democratic Senators had blocked Thomas's nomination, they might have run the risk that Republicans would disclaim culpability for re-creating an all-white Supreme Court if Bush were to have followed Thomas with a white nominee."[1] Others saw the nomination as a provocative invitation to a contentious confirmation process. Accordingly, the Bush administration's strategy in promoting Thomas's confirmation included using Thomas's background of overcoming segregation and discrimination to assert that he would be sensitive to civil rights issues despite his conservative record on them.

Clarence Thomas was born in the segregated South, in the tiny town of Pin Point, Georgia, on June 23, 1948. Until the age of seven, he lived in conditions of poverty with his mother, Leola Williams, and his older sister and younger brother. His father, M.C. Thomas, left the family when the children were very young, and his mother toiled as a domestic worker to support the family. When Thomas turned seven, his mother sent him and his younger brother to live with their grandparents, Myers and Christine Anderson, in nearby Savannah. Myers Anderson's successful small fuel delivery business allowed his family to live more comfortably than most African Americans in the community at that time. Anderson was a hard worker and strict disciplinarian, and he pushed Clarence and his brother to succeed.[2]

Thomas attended segregated parochial schools in Savannah—initially an all-black school (St. Benedict the Moor)—but in 1964, his grandfather enrolled him in an all-white Catholic boarding school, St. John Vianny Minor Seminary. After Thomas graduated from high school in 1967, Anderson, who wanted Thomas to become a priest, sent him to Immaculate Conception Seminary in northwestern Missouri to study for the priesthood. Thomas was subjected to his classmates' racist attitudes in both seminaries, and he subsequently decided against the priesthood. His decision was influenced by a racist remark made by one of his classmates when they learned about the assassination of Dr. Martin Luther King, Jr. In 1968, he left the seminary in Missouri and earned a scholarship to study at the College of the Holy Cross in Worcester, Massachusetts. Thomas majored in English literature, graduating with honors in 1971. In addition to excelling in his studies, he was a member of the track team and was one of the founding members of the Black Student Union.[3]

After graduating from Holy Cross, Thomas earned a scholarship to Yale Law School under its affirmative action program, graduating in 1974. He had hoped to return to Savannah to practice at one of the major law firms, but none of these law firms offered him a position. Thomas subsequently was recruited by Missouri Attorney General John Danforth to work in his office. Thomas accepted this position, and, as assistant attorney general, he was responsible for litigation concerning taxation and similar issues.[4] Danforth would continue to serve as Thomas's mentor for many years.

After Danforth was elected to the United States Senate in 1976, Thomas left the attorney general's office and moved to Monsanto Chemical Company. His work there dealt with environmental law matters, and, after two years of service, he joined Danforth's Senate staff as a legislative assistant. In this position, Thomas became connected to politically active African American conservatives; earlier, he had changed his voter registration from Democrat to Republican.[5] After Ronald Reagan's defeat of incumbent President Jimmy Carter in 1980, Thomas secured a position on the presidential transition team. In 1981 he accepted a position in the new administration as director of the Office for Civil Rights in the Department of Education. Nine months later, he was nominated to become chairman of the Equal Employment Opportunity Commission (EEOC), the federal agency with primary responsibility for enforcing the nation's laws against employment discrimination.[6]

After George H. W. Bush was elected president in 1988, Thomas remained as chairman of the EEOC, but two years later Bush nominated him to serve on the federal Circuit Court of Appeals for the District of Columbia. Ironically, this was the seat previously held by failed nominee Robert Bork, who had resigned in 1988. Despite opposition from some groups, Thomas was confirmed for the Court of Appeals.[7] He had served on that court for about sixteen months when Marshall announced his retirement. In announcing his nomination of Thomas, Bush proclaimed "the fact that he is black and a minority has nothing to do with this in the sense that he is best qualified at this time."[8]

Confirmation Politics

Not surprisingly, Thomas's nomination brought immediate criticism from civil rights groups. Thomas's views on civil rights and racial justice issues were diametrically opposed to those of Thurgood Marshall, the justice whom he would replace on the high court. Moreover, Thomas had spent a large portion of his professional life criticizing the work of traditional civil rights organizations and espousing the policy positions of conservative presidential administrations on a number of civil rights and liberties issues. On the other hand, the nomination was praised by conservative groups who saw Thomas's appointment as a great opportunity to solidify a conservative majority on the Supreme Court which could further repudiate earlier Court rulings, especially on the issue of abortion.

Given these circumstances, it was clear from the outset that this would be a controversial confirmation. In the months preceding the confirmation hearings, Bush administration officials carefully coached Thomas. He watched hours of videotapes of David Souter's confirmation hearings to prepare for his appearance before the Senate Judiciary Committee. Unlike Souter, Thomas had a "paper trail" to deal with, so a decision had to be made about how he should present himself to the Committee. Ultimately, the decision was for Thomas to disavow his earlier record and recast himself in a non-ideological, noncontroversial way.

The hearings began September 10. Following opening statements by Senate Judiciary Committee members, Senator John Danforth officially presented Thomas to the panel. Danforth told the Committee that Thomas possessed special qualities that would make him "an extraordinary justice on the Supreme Court."[9] Thomas testified for five days, from Tuesday, September 10 through Friday, September 13, and again on Monday, September 16. In his opening statement to the Senate Judiciary Committee, Thomas described himself as fair and impartial, and he emphasized that he had no particular ideology or agenda he would bring to the Court.

> It is my hope that when these hearings are completed that this committee will conclude that I am an honest, decent, fair person. I believe that the obligations and responsibilities of a judge, in essence, involve such basic values. A judge must be fair and impartial. A judge must not bring to his job, to the court, the baggage of preconceived notions, of ideology, and certainly not an agenda.[10]

If confirmed, he pledged to "preserve and protect our Constitution and carry with me the values of my heritage: fairness, integrity, openmindedness, honesty, and hard work."[11]

Senators questioned Thomas on a range of issues, including affirmative action, religious liberties, school desegregation, abortion, criminal justice issues, and federalism. On some of these issues, Thomas had taken conservative positions in earlier speeches and writings. His confirmation testimony, however, often was inconsistent with those prior positions. When asked about these inconsistencies, Thomas said that he had advocated certain policy positions when he was an executive branch official, but that things were different in his role as a judge. He implored Committee members to focus their attention primarily on his record on the appellate court. Wisconsin Senator Herbert Kohl, however, challenged this assertion.

> Why is it inappropriate for us to make an evaluation of your candidacy based upon all the things that you have written and said—particularly in view of the fact that you have been on the [appeals] court for only 16 months? If we are going to make an informed judgment on behalf of the American people, why are your policy positions not important?[12]

Thomas again distinguished between his work in the executive branch and his service on the bench.

> When one becomes a judge, the role changes, the roles change. That is why it is different. You are no longer involved in those [policymaking] battles. You are no longer running an agency. You are no longer making policy. You are a judge. It is hard to explain, perhaps,

but you strive—rather than looking for policy positions, you strive for impartiality. You begin to strip down from those policy positions. . . . And I think that is the important message that I am trying to send to you; that yes, my whole record is relevant, but remember that that was as a policy maker not as a judge.[13]

In response to claims that Thomas's record on civil rights showed an insensitivity to issues of discrimination and injustice, his supporters pointed to his background of overcoming poverty and discrimination as evidence that he would be sensitive to these issues on the high court. Thomas echoed these claims during his testimony before the Judiciary Committee.

[G]oing to the Court, the experience I would bring is something I said earlier today, and that is that I feel that since coming from Savannah, from Pin Point, and being in various places in the country, that my journey has not only been a journey geographically, it has also been one demographically.

It has been one that required me to at some point touch on virtually every aspect, every level of our country, from people who couldn't read and write to people who were extremely literate, from people who had no money to people who were very wealthy. So, what I bring to this Court, I believe, is an understanding and ability to stand in the shoes of other people across a broad spectrum of this country.[14]

Some of the most contentious points in the hearings occurred when Thomas was questioned about his views on abortion and the *Roe v. Wade* decision. Despite repeated questions, he refused to reveal his position on this issue. Vermont Senator Patrick Leahy pointed to an earlier speech that Thomas gave to a conservative group in which he praised an article that criticized *Roe* and that called for abortion to be outlawed.[15] Thomas responded that he was merely using the article to persuade conservatives that the particular principles discussed by the article's author could be applied to civil rights issues. In addition to refusing to say whether or not he agreed with *Roe,* Thomas told the panel that he had never even discussed the case.

Following Thomas's appearance, the Committee heard three days of testimony (September 18–20) from witnesses supporting and opposing his confirmation. In the end, Thomas's assertion that he never had discussed *Roe v. Wade,* along with his inconsistent statements about other issues, was troubling to several Judiciary Committee members. As a result, on September 27, the Committee split 7–7 in deciding whether to endorse the nomination. The Committee did, however, vote to send the nomination to the full Senate without a recommendation.[16]

Despite the split vote on the Judiciary Committee and serious opposition by other senators as well, most observers expected the full Senate's action on the nomination to go smoothly. Two days before the final vote was to occur, however, confirmation was temporarily derailed when an allegation of sexual harassment by Thomas became public. National Public Radio reported that Anita Hill, a law professor and former aide to Thomas, alleged that he sexually harassed her when the two worked together in the Department of Education and at the EEOC. Apparently this information had been given to Senator Joseph Biden, Judiciary Committee Chairman, before the end of the hearings, but he failed to inform the Committee immediately about the charges. Democratic Committee members slowly learned about Hill's claims, and, after two reporters broke the story, it was clear that the Committee needed to act on this information.[17]

Senator Biden scheduled a second round of hearings, which began on Friday, October 11. Before the Committee even heard Hill's allegations against him, Thomas began this second phase with an angry statement proclaiming his innocence. After Thomas left the Senate Caucus Room, Hill presented her allegations. In meticulous detail, she told the panel about his "repeated efforts to ask her out on a date, despite her persistence in declining his invitations," and she said that Thomas "insisted on talking about sexual matters, including pornographic films, oral sex, women's breasts, and the size of his own penis."[18] Committee members questioned Hill for several hours about her charges the first day. That evening, Thomas returned to the Committee, categorically denying Hill's allegations and charging that he was the victim of a "high-tech lynching." For the next two days, Committee members continued to grill Hill about her charges, and they heard testimony from other witnesses as well. One panel of four witnesses told the Committee that Hill had confided in each of them about the alleged harassment years before Thomas was nominated to the federal bench. These four witnesses did not know each other, and "each learned about the incidents independently of one another."[19] Several witnesses called in support of Thomas reported that he had never engaged in the behavior Hill described, and others described her as delusional and mentally unstable. Outside of the hearing room, the Committee received information from other women who claimed that Thomas had engaged in sexual harassment at the EEOC, but they were not called to testify.

Several Republican senators, particularly Arlen Specter of Pennsylvania, Orrin Hatch of Utah, and Alan Simpson of Wyoming, accused Hill of outright lying and of being part of a "liberal conspiracy" to defeat Thomas's nomination. Hill was not given any opportunity to respond to these claims, but Thomas returned for a final appearance before the Committee at the end of Hill's testimony. He expressed disgust at having been put through this process but said he "would rather die" than withdraw his name from consideration. The Republican senators went to great lengths to defend Thomas against Hill's charges, but the Democratic senators did not do much to support Hill. As the authors of one study on Thomas noted, "Thomas's angry claim that he was being subjected to a 'high-tech lynching' seemed to put the white senators back on their heels, as if they did not wish to risk any accusations of racial insensitivity by pushing Thomas for answers."[20]

The second round of hearings ended on Sunday night, October 13, and two days later Thomas was confirmed by a vote of 52–48. This was the closest Supreme Court confirmation vote in more than a century. Thomas was sworn in on October 23, 1991.

Media Coverage and Interest Group Participation

Coverage of the Thomas nomination and confirmation by the print media was intense, dramatic, and continual. In the first month after the nomination was announced (July), national newspapers and major regional newspapers ran feature stories, columns, and op-ed pieces nearly every day. Coverage dropped off somewhat during August but increased substantially shortly before the hearings began in September and continued through the second round of proceedings on the Thomas-Hill controversy.[21]

The broadcast media focused considerable attention on the Thomas proceedings, but not on both rounds of hearings. PBS, CNN, C-Span, and Court TV offered live television coverage of the first round, but the major networks (ABC, CBS, NBC) simply reported on the hearings on their evening news shows. CNN covered the nomination announcement in a live broadcast, and ABC News Nightline ran three specials—one on the day of the announcement and the other during two days of hearings. The second round, focusing on Anita Hill's sexual harassment allegations, did generate live television coverage by the major networks, however. ABC, NBC, and CBS presented live coverage of nine hours of testimony on the first day of round two and limited additional coverage in the following days.[22]

While a much smaller number of interest groups testified during David Souter's confirmation hearings than during Robert Bork's, the number increased dramatically with the Thomas hearings. The Senate Judiciary Committee heard testimony from nearly fifty groups, almost two to one in opposition to confirmation. Groups opposing confirmation generally focused on his record on civil liberties and civil rights issues, including women's reproductive rights.

Groups Testifying Against Confirmation

Society of American Law Teachers

Lawyers' Committee for Civil Rights Under Law

National Women's Law Center

Women's Legal Defense Fund

National Abortion Rights Action League

Planned Parenthood

AFL-CIO

People for the American Way Action Fund

NAACP Legal Defense and Educational Fund

Leadership Conference on Civil Rights

Mexican-American Legal Defense and Education Fund

Alliance for Justice

Coalition of Black Trade Unionists

National Bar Association (45% against, 44% in favor)

National Conference of Black Lawyers

National Asian Pacific-American Bar Association

National Black Police Association

National Council of Senior Citizens

NAACP

National Baptist Convention, U.S.A., Inc.

Progressive National Baptist Convention

National Women's Political Caucus

National Organization for Women (NOW)

Fund for the Feminist Majority

NOW Legal Defense and Education Fund

American Association of University Women

National Black Women's Health Project

Supreme Court Watch

Center for Constitutional Rights

Americans for Democratic Action

National Association of Criminal Defense Lawyers

Representatives of the ABA Standing Committee on the Federal Judiciary testified in favor of confirmation. They reported that the Committee had given Thomas a rating of qualified, with two members in dissent and one recusal. Other groups supporting confirmation focused primarily on Thomas's personal history of overcoming poverty and discrimination, his record on criminal justice issues, and his integrity and belief in basic values of self-discipline and hard work.

Groups Testifying in Favor of Confirmation

ABA Standing Committee on the Federal Judiciary

Citizens for Law and Order

National Black Nurses Association

National Center for Neighborhood Enterprise

Zeta Phi Beta Sorority, Inc.

Council of 100

Agudath Israel of America

Heartland Coalition (created specifically in response to civil rights groups' opposition
   to Thomas)

National Law Enforcement Council

National Sheriffs' Association

National Troopers Coalition

International Association of Chiefs of Police

Washington Legal Foundation

Concerned Women for America

Montgomery County (Maryland) Black Republican Council

Republican Black Caucus

Professional Bail Agents

Judicial Performance

Based on his testimony before the Senate Judiciary Committee, one might have
expected Thomas to be a moderate justice. This has not been the case, however.
Thomas was a strong conservative in his first term, and he has not wavered in the
years since then. His voting record and judicial opinions illustrate that Thomas is
one of the most conservative justices currently serving on the Court.

Voting Behavior

During his first ten terms on the Court, Thomas has been aligned most consistently with the Court's two most conservative members—Justice Antonin Scalia
and Chief Justice William Rehnquist. During his very first term (1991–1992), in
nonunanimous decisions, Thomas voted with Justice Scalia 79% of the time and
with Chief Justice Rehnquist 72% of the time. Conversely, he voted with the

Court's two most liberal members, Justices Blackmun and Stevens, in only 28% and 26% of the split decisions, respectively.[23]

Data for subsequent terms indicate similar patterns. For example, in the Court's civil rights and civil liberties cases for the 1992–1993 through 2000–2001 terms, Thomas voted for a conservative outcome in 73% of the cases, with the highest score at 82% for the 1997–1998 term and the lowest score at 68% just one term earlier.[24] According to the *Harvard Law Review*'s annual statistics, for all written opinions from the 1995–1996 through 1999–2000 terms, Thomas had the highest agreement with Justice Scalia (89%) and Chief Justice Rehnquist (81%), and he voted least often with Justice Stevens (46%). Results for nonunanimous cases for the three terms from 1997–1998 to 1999–2000 are similar; Thomas voted most frequently with Scalia (75%) and least often with Stevens (16%).[25]

Civil Rights

As indicated earlier, much of the opposition directed at Thomas by civil rights groups was because of the conservative positions that he had taken in a number of speeches and articles on a range of racial discrimination issues. He had been very critical of affirmative action, for example, arguing that "[g]oals and timetables, long a popular rallying cry among some who claim to be concerned with the right to equal employment opportunity, have become a sideshow in the war on discrimination."[26] During his confirmation hearings, however, Thomas appeared to back away from his strong criticism of affirmative action. In an exchange with Delaware Senator Joseph Biden, Thomas noted:

> I have initiated affirmative action programs. I have supported affirmative action programs. Whether or not I agree with all of them I think is a matter of record. But the fact that I don't agree with all of them does not mean that I am not a supporter of the underlying effort. I am and have been my entire adult life.[27]

Biden asked for clarification, that is, whether Thomas approved of affirmative action programs that are not based on race. Thomas replied, "I said that from a policy standpoint I agreed with affirmative action policies that focused on disadvantaged minorities and disadvantaged individuals in our society.[28]

In the only substantive affirmative action case decided since Thomas's arrival on the Court, his views most closely resemble those taken when he was an executive branch official. In *Adarand Constructors v. Pena* (1995), a 5–4 majority ruled that affirmative action programs established by the federal government could be upheld only if they met "strict scrutiny," that is, they must be narrowly tailored to achieve a compelling interest. Justice O'Connor's majority opinion noted nonetheless that "[t]he unhappy persistence of both the practice and the lingering effects of racial discrimination against minority groups in this country is an unfortunate reality, and government is not disqualified from acting in response to it."[29] *Adarand* reversed the Court's earlier decision in *Metro Broadcasting v. FCC* (1990), which had held that affirmative action programs of the federal government would be subjected to "intermediate scrutiny," a lesser standard, while strict scrutiny would apply only to such programs by state and local governments. While agreeing that strict scrutiny applied to all government affirmative action programs based on race, Thomas wrote a concurring opinion in which he attacked government affirmative action programs as racial paternalism.

> So-called "benign" discrimination teaches many [whites] that because of chronic and apparently immutable handicaps, minorities cannot compete with them without their patronizing indulgence. Inevitably, such programs engender attitudes of superiority or, alternatively, provoke resentment among those who believe that they have been wronged by the government's use of race. The programs stamp minorities with a badge of inferiority and may cause them to develop dependencies or to adopt an attitude that they are "entitled" to preference.[30]

Before his nomination to the Court, Thomas also was critical of the Court's voting rights jurisprudence. In a 1988 speech he stated, "Unfortunately, many of the Court's decisions in the area of voting rights presuppose that blacks, whites, Hispanics, and other ethnic groups will inevitably vote in blocs. Instead of looking at the right to vote as an individual right, the Court has regarded the right as protected when the individual racial or ethnic group has sufficient clout."[31] Thomas provided a blistering attack on the Court's interpretation of the Voting Rights Act of 1965 in *Holder v. Hall* (1994),[32] a case involving a claim of minority vote dilution. Minority vote dilution is "a process whereby election laws or practices, either singly or in concert, combine with systematic bloc voting among an identifiable group to dominate or cancel the voting strength of at least one minority group."[33] Minority vote dilution occurred as a result of the success of the Voting Rights Act in increasing voter registration and voter participation by African Americans who had been effectively disenfranchised by the policies and practices of state and local governments in the South. The high court had to develop a standard for deciding vote dilution cases. The Warren Court ruled that litigants claiming vote dilution could base their claims on a showing of either a discriminatory purpose or a discriminatory effect. The Burger Court initially accepted the adverse effect standard as sufficient in a 1973 case, *White v. Regester*. In *Mobile v. Bolden* decided seven years later, however, the Burger Court rejected the adverse effect standard, ruling that litigants claiming vote dilution must prove a discriminatory purpose or intent. But in an amendment to the Voting Rights Act in 1982, Congress reinstituted the adverse effect standard as sufficient for bringing vote dilution claims, and the Court upheld this standard in a 1986 case, *Thornburgh v. Gingles*.

In *Holder,* Thomas joined a five-member majority in ruling that the size of a governing body is not subject to a vote dilution claim under the Voting Rights Act. He issued a separate concurrence contending that the Voting Rights Act was not meant to deal with matters of vote dilution or districting systems. He said that the language in the Act was directed only at "practices that affect minority citizens's access to the ballot."[34] Moreover, he called for *Thornburgh* to be overruled. In very strong language near the end of his opinion, Thomas emphatically stated his displeasure with existing precedents:

> In my view, our current practice should not continue. Not for another Term, not until the next case, not for another day. The disastrous implications of the policies we have adopted under the Act are too grave; the dissembling in our approach to the Act too damaging to the credibility of the federal judiciary. The "inherent tension"—indeed, I would call it an irreconcilable conflict—between the standards we have adopted for evaluating vote dilution claims and the text of the Voting Rights Act would itself be sufficient in my view to warrant overruling the interpretation of Sect. 2 [of the Act] set out in *[Thornburg v.] Gingles.* When that obvious conflict is combined with the destructive effects our expansive reading of the Act has had in involving the federal judiciary in the project of dividing the Nation into racially segregated electoral districts, I can see no reasonable alternative to abandoning our unfortunate understanding of the Act.[35]

This opinion appears to contradict his testimony before the Judiciary Committee. When asked by Massachusetts Senator Edward Kennedy whether he supported the decisions in *Thornburg* and a related case *(White v. Regester),* Thomas replied, "I absolutely support the aggressive enforcement of voting rights laws and certainly support the results in those cases."[36]

Since arriving on the Court, Thomas also has expressed his belief that redistricting plans which create so-called majority-minority districts are unconstitutional. In *Shaw v. Reno* (1993), a group of white voters in North Carolina challenged the creation of two majority-black congressional districts. Thomas joined a majority ruling which held that equal protection challenges to these plans must be examined under strict scrutiny.[37] Under this standard, such plans can be upheld only if they are narrowly tailored to achieve a compelling interest. This decision helped to spur additional litigation challenging majority-minority congressional districts in other states. Two terms after *Shaw,* in a case from Georgia, the Court ruled that when race is the predominant factor in drawing district lines, strict scrutiny applies.[38] Two years later, the justices used strict scrutiny to invalidate four majority-minority districts, one in North Carolina *(Shaw v. Hunt)* and three in Texas *(Bush v. Vera).*[39] In *Shaw v. Hunt,* by a 5–4 vote, the Court held that race was the predominant factor in drawing the challenged congressional district and that the plan was not narrowly tailored to achieve a compelling interest. In *Bush v. Vera,* five justices agreed that the challenged districts were invalid, but there was no majority opinion. Justices O'Connor, Rehnquist, and Kennedy examined the districts under strict scrutiny only after concluding that race was the predominant factor in drawing them. In a separate opinion joined by Justice Scalia, Thomas maintained that there was no need to determine whether race was the predominant factor; the intentional creation of majority-minority districts automatically triggers strict scrutiny. Thomas wrote, "I am content to reaffirm our holding in *Adarand* that all racial classifications by government must be strictly scrutinized and, even in the sensitive area of state legislative redistricting, I would make no exceptions."[40]

Redistricting in North Carolina returned to the Court's agenda in the 2000–2001 term. The North Carolina legislature reconfigured the congressional district that had been challenged and then struck down in the earlier *Shaw* cases, but a lower federal court again held that the district resulted from an unconstitutional racial gerrymander. In a 5–4 decision in *Hunt v. Cromartie* (2001), the justices upheld the new plan.[41] Writing for the majority, Justice Breyer said that although race was a factor in drawing the district, it was not the predominant one. In addition, Breyer concluded that when race is strongly correlated with party affiliation, majority-minority districts are not necessarily evidence of unconstitutional racial gerrymandering. Justice Thomas's dissent, joined by Chief Justice Rehnquist and Justices Scalia and Kennedy, contended that the majority should have deferred to the lower court's findings. Moreover, he emphasized that "racial gerrymandering offends the Constitution whether the motivation is malicious or benign," and also observed that "it is not a defense that the Legislature merely may have drawn the district based on the stereotype that blacks are reliable Democratic voters."[42]

While the Court has not heard many school desegregation cases since Thomas's appointment, two cases have provided Thomas the opportunity to express his views on this issue. The first, *United States v. Fordice* (1992), decided in his first term, involved desegregation in higher education.[43] Here the Court ruled that although Mississippi had ended its policy of *de jure* segregation of its colleges and universities, its current admissions policies perpetuated segregation in those institutions, and this problem had to be remedied. Thomas wrote a brief concurrence that emphasized his support for the continuing existence of historically black institutions of higher education. "It would be ironic . . . if the institutions that sustained blacks during segregation were themselves destroyed in an effort to combat its vestiges."[44]

Three years after *Fordice*, Thomas joined Chief Justice Rehnquist's majority holding that in school desegregation cases, federal judges' remedial authority is limited to remedying the vestiges of past discrimination (*Missouri v. Jenkins*, 1995).[45] Here a federal district judge had issued several orders designed to improve inner-city schools so that white suburban students would attend them and "white flight" could be diminished. Thomas agreed that the judge had overstepped his authority, and he added a sharp concurrence alleging paternalism on the part of the district judge. "It never ceases to amaze me that the courts are so willing to assume that anything that is predominantly black must be inferior. Instead of focusing on remedying the harm done to those black schoolchildren injured by segregation, the District Court sought to convert the Kansas City, Missouri, School District (KCMSD) into a 'magnet district' that would reverse the 'white flight' caused by desegregation."[46] Thomas went further; he attacked the *Brown v. Board of Education* (1954) decision. In a footnote in *Brown,* Chief Justice Warren made reference to social science studies that demonstrated the negative impact of segregation on African American school children. Thomas wrote, "the court has read our cases to support the theory that black students suffer an unspecified psychological harm from segregation that retards their mental and educational development. This approach relies on questionable social science research rather than constitutional principle, but it also rests on an assumption of African American inferiority."[47]

Abortion

Despite Thomas's refusal to answer the Judiciary Committee's questions about abortion and his claim that he never had discussed the landmark *Roe* decision, most legal experts predicted that he would vote to overrule *Roe* and return all abortion matters to states to decide. At the end of his first term, these predictions came true. By a 5–4 vote, with Justices O'Connor, Kennedy, and Souter jointly writing the controlling opinion, the Court refused to overturn *Roe,* although it was modified in a way that permits greater restrictions on abortion (*Planned Parenthood v. Casey,* 1992).[48] Thomas joined opinions by Chief Justice Rehnquist and Justice Scalia explicitly calling for *Roe* to be overturned. The Court, according to Rehnquist, "was mistaken in *Roe* when it classified a woman's decision to terminate her pregnancy as a 'fundamental right' that could be abridged only in a manner which withstood 'strict scrutiny.'"[49] Scalia asserted that women do not have a constitutional right to abortion because "the Constitution says absolutely nothing about it," and "longstanding traditions of American society have permitted it to be legally proscribed."[50]

If there were any lingering doubts about Thomas's views on abortion, they were cleared up eight years later when the justices decided a case concerning so-called "partial birth abortion." This term, created by abortion opponents, refers to an abortion procedure used primarily in second-trimester abortions (before viability) in which the fetus is aborted after it has been partially delivered.[51] In *Stenberg v. Carhart* (2000), a narrow majority invalidated Nebraska's ban on "partial birth abortion."[52] In his majority opinion, Justice Breyer said that because the statute prohibited one abortion procedure that was safer for women than other procedures in some circumstances, it posed an undue burden in violation of *Casey*. In addition, the law did not contain an exception for preserving the health of the mother. In his dissent, joined by Chief Justice Rehnquist and Justice Scalia, Thomas wrote:

> Today's decision is so obviously irreconcilable with *Casey's* explication of what its undue-burden standard requires, let alone the Constitution, that it should be seen for what it is, a reinstitution of the pre-*Webster* abortion-on-demand era in which the mere invocation of "abortion rights" trumps any contrary societal interest. If this statute is unconstitutional under *Casey*, then *Casey* meant nothing at all, and the Court should candidly admit it.[53]

According to Thomas, *Casey* requires a health exception only if the mother's life or health is endangered by the pregnancy itself; it does not apply to the procedure to be used.

Federalism and Commerce Powers

Thomas has given some attention to federalism and commerce powers in his Supreme Court opinions. In recent years, the Court's agenda has included a number of cases involving questions about the proper relationship between the federal government and the states in our constitutional system and about the extent of congressional powers in regulating commerce. Several cases in these areas have dramatically altered interpretations that were thought to be settled. They generally involve debates between two interpretations: cooperative federalism and dual federalism. Cooperative federalism emphasizes a federal system based on national supremacy, while dual federalism is based on the principle that the national government and the states are co-equal sovereigns.

Thomas provided an extensive explanation of his interpretation of federalism in a case concerning term limits. In *U.S. Term Limits v. Thornton* (1995), the Court ruled that the Constitution prohibits states from imposing term limits on their congressional representatives. Justice Stevens's majority opinion construed the power of the national government as stemming from the people of the nation rather than from the individual states, and he rejected the proposition that the Tenth Amendment reserved powers to the states to set qualifications for members of Congress. His opinion endorsed cooperative federalism as the proper understanding of the federal system created by the founders of the Constitution.

> The Framers decided that the qualifications for service in the Congress of the United States be fixed in the Constitution and be uniform throughout the Nation. That decision reflects the Framers' understanding that Members of Congress are chosen by separate constituencies, but that they become, when elected, servants of the people of the United States. They are not merely delegates appointed by separate, sovereign states; they occupy offices that are integral and essential components of a singly National Government. In the

absence of a properly passed constitutional amendment, allowing individual States to craft their own qualifications for Congress would thus erode the structure envisioned by the Framers.[54]

By contrast, Thomas's dissent supported dual federalism. He stressed that "[t]he ultimate source of the Constitution's authority is the consent of the people of each individual State, not the consent of the undifferentiated people of the Nation as a whole."[55]He also interpreted the Tenth Amendment as providing for significant authority to states, including the power to determine qualifications for their congressional representatives.

While dual federalism did not prevail in *U.S. Term Limits,* two years later a narrow majority endorsed this approach. This case involved the Brady Handgun Violence Prevention Act, which required the United States Attorney General to create a national database providing for instant background checks before individuals could purchase handguns. Because it would take time to establish such a database, the law contained other provisions for conducting background checks in the meantime. Under the Act, firearm dealers were permitted to sell guns to individuals who already held a state handgun permit or who lived in states that already had instant background check systems. If neither of these conditions was met, the law required that state and local law enforcement officers conduct background checks on potential buyers. Two local sheriffs challenged the latter provisions, claiming that the national government could not place such a mandate on state and local officials. A divided Court agreed with their claims in *Printz v. United States* (1997). Thomas joined Justice Scalia's majority opinion which endorsed the dual federalism approach. Scalia concluded that neither historical practices nor the structure of the Constitution permitted Congress to direct state and local officials to participate in this regulatory program. He maintained that "such commands are fundamentally incompatible with our constitutional system of dual sovereignty."[56] In addition to suggesting that the Second Amendment protects an individual's right to bear arms, Thomas's brief concurrence stressed that "the Tenth Amendment affirms the undeniable notion that under our Constitution, the Federal Government is one of enumerated, hence limited powers. Accordingly, the Federal Government may act only where the Constitution authorizes it to do so."[57]

Thomas also joined the conservative majority in three subsequent cases in 1999 that upheld state sovereignty over the powers of the national government. In *Alden v. Maine,* by a 5–4 vote, the Court ruled that state employees could not file suits in state courts for enforcement of the overtime pay provisions of the federal Fair Labor Standards Act.[58] In the other two cases, the same majority held that states cannot be sued for either trademark infringement or patent infringement.[59] Thomas was in the majority in two additional rulings in 2000 and 2001 that expanded states' immunity from lawsuits. In one case the Court decided that state employees may not sue their employer for violations of the federal Age Discrimination and Employment Act, and in the other the holding was that those employees may not sue for damages for state violations of the federal Americans with Disabilities Act.[60]

In addition to significant decisions involving federalism with respect to term limits, gun control, and state immunity from lawsuits, in recent years the Court has issued important rulings regarding the extent of federal authority to regulate commerce. Under the Commerce Clause in Article I, Section 8 of the Constitution, Congress has the power "To regulate Commerce with foreign Nations, and among the several States, and with the Indian Tribes." Based on this Clause, Congress has the power to regulate commerce between the states—interstate commerce—but not commerce that occurs solely within a state's borders—intrastate commerce. In the late nineteenth and early twentieth centuries, the Court took a narrow view of congressional power to regulate interstate commerce. For example, in 1918, the justices invalidated the Federal Child Labor Act, a law that attempted to regulate child labor by prohibiting the interstate shipment of goods made in factories that employed children under a certain age.[61] The majority held that the law was an unconstitutional exercise of congressional authority because mining and manufacturing were not transactions in interstate commerce, but were matters that must be left to the states to regulate. Between 1933 and 1936, the Court used this precedent to strike down several pieces of New Deal legislation that were based on congressional authority under the Commerce Clause. Beginning in 1937, however, the Court rejected this narrow interpretation of the Commerce Clause and ruled that Congress had broad authority to regulate a variety of economic activities, including those that seemed to some to be only remotely connected to interstate commerce.

Following this reinterpretation of the Commerce Clause in the late 1930s and early 1940s, the Court did not again invalidate a congressional exercise of commerce power until 1976. In *National League of Cities v. Usery,* a divided Court ruled that Congress had overstepped its commerce authority when it applied the wage and hour provisions of the federal Fair Labor Standards Act to state and local governments.[62] In 1985, however, the Court reversed this precedent, holding that state and local governments must abide by this federal law *(Garcia v. San Antonio Metropolitan Transit Authority).*

In a surprising development in 1995, the Court rejected the broad interpretation of the Commerce Clause that had been accepted after the New Deal and applied consistently (except for *National League of Cities*) since then. In *United States v. Lopez,* the Court struck down by a 5–4 vote the Gun-Free School Zones Act of 1990 on the grounds that Congress had not shown that gun violence in schools has a substantial effect on interstate commerce.[63] Though he joined the majority opinion, Thomas wrote a lone concurrence contending that the pre-New Deal interpretation of the Commerce Clause which strictly limited congressional power was more consistent with the intentions of the framers of the Constitution.

> At the time the original Constitution was ratified, "commerce" consisted of selling, buying, and bartering, as well as transporting for these purposes. . . . The term "commerce" was used in contradistinction to productive activities such as manufacturing and agriculture. . . . [Manufactured] parts may come from different States or other nations and hence may have been in the flow of commerce at one time, but manufacturing takes place at a discrete site. Agriculture and manufacturing involve the production of goods; commerce encompasses traffic in such articles.[64]

He did not call for an immediate change in the Court's approach, however, noting that although he was "willing to return to the original understanding" of the Commerce Clause, "many believe that it is too late in the day to undertake a fundamental reexamination of the past 60 years."[65]

Not surprisingly, then, Thomas was part of a five-member majority in *United States v. Morrison* (2000) that utilized *Lopez* to invalidate a provision of the Violence Against Women Act of 1994.[66] Under this provision, victims of gender-motivated violence were permitted to sue their attackers in federal court. While the law was based on congressional findings about the effects of violence against women on interstate commerce, the majority ruled that gender-motivated violence was not an economic activity, nor did it have a substantial effect on interstate commerce. Referring to the substantial effects test as a "rootless and malleable standard," Thomas's concurring opinion emphasized that it is "inconsistent with the original understanding of Congress's powers and with th[e] Court's early Commerce Clause cases."[67]

Criminal Justice

Another area in which Thomas's conservatism is very apparent is criminal justice, especially in cases dealing with the death penalty and with prisoners' rights under the Eighth Amendment. Concerns about federalism also appear to influence his decisions in some of these cases. In his first term, Thomas wrote an opinion that harshly criticized the Court for applying the Eighth Amendment's Cruel and Unusual Punishments Clause to protect prisoners. The case involved an inmate who was severely beaten by prison guards while handcuffed and shackled, while the supervisor watched the incident and reportedly told the guards "not to have too much fun." Although the beating resulted in severe bruises, bleeding, loosened teeth, and a cracked partial dental plate, a federal appellate court rejected the inmate's civil damages suit, determining that the injuries were minor and that he needed to prove significant injury in order to proceed with the suit. With only Justices Thomas and Scalia in dissent, the Court ruled in *Hudson v. McMillian* (1992) that the inmate did not need to prove a "significant injury," but the appropriate standard for the courts was to determine "whether [physical] force was applied in a good-faith effort to maintain or restore discipline, or [was applied] maliciously and sadistically to cause harm."[68] In a sharp dissent, Thomas wrote:

> Today's expansion of the Cruel and Unusual Punishment Clause beyond all bounds of history and precedent is, I suspect, yet another manifestation of the pervasive view that the Federal Constitution must address all ills in our society. Abusive behavior by prison guards is deplorable conduct that properly evokes outrage and contempt. But that does not mean that it is invariably unconstitutional. The Eighth Amendment is not, and should not be turned into, a National Code of Prison Regulation.[69]

One year later, Thomas argued that the Eighth Amendment applies only to the sentencing decision, not to prisoners' claims concerning the conditions of confinement, excessive force, or other incarceration issues (*Helling v. McKinney*, 1993). In Thomas's view, these matters are to be left to state legislatures and executives to decide.

With respect to the death penalty, Thomas has joined the conservatives in decisions limiting federal court review of habeas corpus petitions by inmates on death row.[70] He dissented from a 1994 decision authorizing federal district judges to delay executions until death-row inmates obtain legal representation for final habeas challenges to their convictions and sentences *(McFarland v. Scott)*.[71] The case concerned the interpretation of a statute entitling death row inmates to receive the assistance of counsel in the habeas corpus process. The lower court had ruled that counsel was not required under the law until after the habeas petition had been filed and that federal judges were not permitted to stay executions in the meantime. According to Justice Blackmun's majority opinion, "Requiring an indigent capital petitioner to proceed without counsel in order to obtain counsel would thus expose him to the substantial risk that his habeas claims never would be heard on the merits."[72] Thomas, joined by Chief Justice Rehnquist and Justice Scalia, agreed with the lower court's conclusion.

Thomas dissented from two decisions in 2001 regarding jury instructions in capital sentencing proceedings. In *Penry v. Johnson,* the Court decided by a 6–3 vote that a trial judge's supplemental instruction concerning mitigating evidence of the defendant's mental retardation and childhood abuse was not constitutionally adequate.[73] Joined by Chief Justice Rehnquist, Thomas dissented, asserting that the trial court had given the jurors an adequate opportunity to consider the mitigating evidence presented by the defendant. The justices ruled by a 7–2 vote in *Shafer v. South Carolina* that "whenever future dangerousness is at issue in a capital sentencing proceeding . . . due process requires that the jury be informed that a life sentence carries no possibility of parole."[74] Thomas's dissent declared that the instructions regarding life imprisonment provided sufficient information to the jury. Moreover, he warned that "it is not this Court's role to micromanage state sentencing proceedings or to develop model jury instructions," and he accused the majority of "interfer[ing]. . . with matters that the Constitution leaves to the States."[75]

Church-State Issues

On matters involving alleged violations of the Establishment Clause, Thomas regularly has joined with accommodationist Justices Rehnquist and Scalia, who assert that the Constitution permits government support of religion as long as this is done on a nonpreferential basis. During his first term, Thomas joined Justice Scalia's dissent castigating the majority for holding that school-sponsored prayers at public school graduation ceremonies violated the Establishment Clause (*Lee v. Weisman*, 1992). In similar fashion eight years later, he joined Chief Justice Rehnquist's acerbic dissent from the ruling that struck down school-sponsored, student-led prayers at public high school football games (*Santa Fe Independent School District v. Doe*, 2000).

Thomas provided his interpretation of the history of the Establishment Clause in a case from 1995, *Rosenberger v. University of Virginia*. Here, a bitterly divided Court ruled that a university's funding for a religious publication produced by a student group would not violate the Establishment Clause.[76] Thomas, in a separate concurrence, alleged that the framers of the Constitution did not intend to prohibit government support for religion. In 2000, he wrote a plurality opinion upholding a federal program that used public funds to purchase computers and other instructional materials for religious schools *(Mitchell v. Helms)*.[77] He concluded that there was no constitutional violation because the funds were provided in neutral,and nondiscriminatory ways to both religious and nonreligious schools. In addition, Thomas asserted that the aid could be diverted later to religious purposes without constituting an establishment violation. Justices O'Connor and Breyer concurred only in the judgment, rejecting Thomas's interpretation of neutrality in these types of cases. A year later, Thomas wrote for the majority when the Court ruled that a public school could not refuse to allow a religious group to use its building facilities for an after-school religious program for elementary school students (*Good News Club v. Milford Central School*, 2001).[78] Because other groups were permitted to hold after-school meetings, Thomas said that the school had violated the Good News Club's free speech rights by engaging in viewpoint discrimination. He also found no Establishment Clause violation.

General Judicial Philosophy

Thomas's consistently conservative performance on the Supreme Court can be explained in part by his judicial philosophy. He advocates limiting judicial involvement in policy making, deferring to decisions made by elected officials, limiting the scope of constitutional rights, and transferring powers away from the national government to the states, where he thinks they legitimately belong. Thomas, like Robert Bork, is an advocate of "original intent jurisprudence," of interpreting the Constitution strictly according to the intentions of the framers. In Thomas's view, this approach will ensure that judges are "kept within their proper sphere of authority and thereby cease usurping the power of other governmental branches and intruding on the autonomy of state governments."[79]

Summary

When President George H.W. Bush nominated Clarence Thomas to succeed Thurgood Marshall in 1991, conservatives in the Bush administration and elsewhere were hopeful that he would become a strong and dependable conservative voice on the Court. He has in fact fulfilled their hopes and expectations. Through his votes and opinions, Thomas has taken positions that reflect the views of conservatives on a range of important issues, including affirmative action, abortion, federalism, criminal justice and church-state matters. While David Souter proved to be a "strikeout" for conservatives, Clarence Thomas clearly is the "home-run" that they had hoped for.

CHAPTER FOUR

Ruth Bader Ginsburg

"A Judge's Judge and a Lawyer's Lawyer"

After the relative calm of David Souter's confirmation proceedings, the controversy surrounding Clarence Thomas's confirmation had reignited concerns about the nomination and confirmation process for Supreme Court justices. But by the time the next vacancy occurred, a Democratic president was in office after twelve continuous years of Republican administrations. This was the first appointment to the Supreme Court made by a Democratic president since President Lyndon Johnson's nomination of Thurgood Marshall, the first African American justice, a quarter of a century earlier. While President Jimmy Carter made hundreds of appointments to the lower federal courts, he did not have the opportunity to appoint a single Supreme Court justice.

When Justice Byron White announced in March of 1993 that he would retire at the end of the term, President Clinton had his first opportunity to affect the composition of the Court. Although he had been appointed by Democratic President John F. Kennedy, White became a conservative on the Court, particularly in civil rights and liberties cases. For example, while initially supportive of civil rights, especially legal efforts to promote school desegregation, he became a vigorous opponent of affirmative action. White issued a passionate dissent from *Roe v. Wade* (1973), the decision establishing a woman's right to abortion, and his opposition to that ruling continued until his retirement. In First Amendment freedom of speech and press cases, he generally voted to uphold government regulations, and in Establishment Clause cases, he usually ruled in favor of policies claimed to be church-state violations.[1]

As expected, Court observers speculated about who White's successor would be. Would President Clinton choose a moderate, non-controversial nominee to avoid a contentious confirmation battle, or would he select someone with a strong liberal record in hopes of moving the Court in a more liberal direction? Shortly after Justice White announced his retirement, Clinton said he was interested in appointing a justice with political experience and a "big heart" and indicated he would not limit his list of potential nominees to sitting judges, as his predecessors had done. In addition to focusing on merit considerations—legal experience, intellectual ability, and judicial temperament—he specifically noted that he would look for candidates who were pro-choice on abortion.[2]

It took nearly three months for President Clinton to make a decision on this appointment, a delay for which he endured heavy criticism. His initial list of potential candidates numbered over forty and included both politicians and judges. Clinton aides reported that Mario Cuomo, then Governor of New York, Secretary of Education Richard Riley, and Secretary of the Interior Bruce Babbitt were high on the list, but for a variety of reasons all three declined to accept the nomination. Several federal judges also were high on the list. After much consideration, Clinton turned to Stephen Breyer, chief judge of the First U.S. Circuit Court of Appeals in Boston. Breyer was well respected by senators from both political parties for his work as counsel to the Senate Judiciary Committee, and he likely would have been confirmed with ease. But after meeting with Breyer, Clinton still was undecided. The decision not to appoint Breyer unleashed more criticism, however, because Clinton aides already had leaked Breyer's name as the likely choice. Subsequently, Clinton met with Ruth Bader Ginsburg, a judge on the prestigious U.S. Court of Appeals for the District of Columbia. During this meeting, he was moved by Ginsburg's life story, of how she overcame pervasive sex discrimination in the legal profession and became an important advocate for equality before the law as well as a respected federal judge.[3]

On Monday, June 14, 1993 in a Rose Garden ceremony, President Clinton presented Judge Ruth Bader Ginsburg to the media, describing her as "one of our nation's best judges, progressive in outlook, wise in judgment, balanced and fair in her opinions," and he said that she would "be a force for consensus-building on the Supreme Court."[4] In general, the nomination was met with high praise and enthusiasm, but there also were some critics. On the one hand, conservative groups claimed that Ginsburg would become a judicial activist. Conversely, liberal organizations expressed concern that her cautious, technical approach to the law would make her less likely to join with liberals to reverse the tide of conservative rulings. Anti-choice groups criticized Ginsburg because of her support for abortion rights, but pro-choice advocates were disturbed by her statements which were somewhat critical of the 1973 *Roe v. Wade* decision. Ginsburg had suggested that, rather than relying on the right of privacy to recognize a woman's right to abortion, perhaps the Court should have used the Equal Protection Clause of the Fourteenth Amendment. She also had observed that before *Roe* was decided, several states had begun to reform their abortion laws, but the broad decision in *Roe* preempted further state action which may have been more effective in securing abortion rights in the long run. Despite criticisms by some groups, legal experts predicted she would be confirmed unless something extraordinary occurred during the hearings.

Ginsburg's life story is a remarkable one, as countless legal experts and other commentators have pointed out. Ruth Joan Bader was born on March 15, 1933 in Brooklyn, New York, the second daughter of Nathan and Celia Bader. She attended public schools in Brooklyn and after high school graduation enrolled at Cornell University, where she majored in government. She graduated Phi Beta Kappa from Cornell in 1954. Shortly after graduation, Ruth Bader married Martin Ginsburg, a classmate at Cornell who had begun studies at Harvard Law School while she finished her senior year. Sometime during that year, Martin Ginsburg was drafted into the armed services, and they were stationed in Oklahoma for two years. She applied for a GS-5 position in the Social Security office there, and, although her score on the civil service exam made her eligible for this position, she was assigned to a GS-2 typist job after she told the personnel officer that she was pregnant.[5]

Once Martin Ginsburg's military obligations were completed in 1956, both Ginsburgs enrolled in Harvard Law School. Ruth Ginsburg's excellent academic performance earned her a place on the prestigious Law Review. This is especially impressive, given her child care responsibilities and the blatant discrimination to which she and the other eight women in her class were subjected. The Dean of the Law School reportedly accused the women of taking seats that should have gone to men.[6]

In 1958, when Martin Ginsburg graduated from law school and took a position with a law firm in New York, Ruth Ginsburg was able to continue her law studies at Columbia University, where she again made Law Review and was tied for first in her class. Gender discrimination in the legal field was so pervasive that, despite her excellent credentials, upon graduation in 1959 she received no job offers from the top Manhattan firms. In addition, although impressed by her record, Supreme Court Justice Felix Frankfurter turned her down for a clerkship, allegedly because he was not yet ready to hire a woman. She later described her predicament this way: "I had three strikes against me. To be a woman, a Jew, and a mother to boot. That combination was a bit too much."[7] Ginsburg did serve as a clerk to Federal District Judge Edmund Palmieri, 1961–1963, after which she was contacted by Columbia University to participate in a comparative legal systems project. This project permitted her to study in Sweden, and she later wrote two books on Swedish law which became standard works on the subject. In 1963, Ginsburg became the second woman on the law faculty at Rutgers University, where she taught constitutional law and the conflict of laws until 1972.[8]

During her time at Rutgers, Ginsburg's awareness of gender discrimination increased on both a personal and a societal level. When she became pregnant with her second child, she concealed the pregnancy by wearing baggy clothes to make sure that it would not prevent her from receiving tenure the way her first pregnancy had limited her employment with the civil service. After she agreed to student requests to develop a course on feminist law, Ginsburg was appalled by the paucity of materials available on this subject and the blatant sexism of what was available. On a broader level, she joined the staff of the New Jersey American Civil Liberties Union (ACLU) to assist in gender discrimination litigation, specifically a case involving schoolteachers who had lost their positions when they became pregnant. Her work on this case impressed Melvin Wulf, national legal director of the ACLU, and he asked her to join the national staff in preparing arguments for a major gender discrimination case, *Reed v. Reed* (1971), that was about to be heard by the U.S. Supreme Court. They were successful in persuading the Court, for the first time, to declare a state law unconstitutional because of gender discrimination.[9]

After the *Reed* decision, the ACLU established the Women's Rights Project to handle more gender discrimination litigation, and the board of directors chose Ginsburg as its first director. By this time, she had joined the faculty at Columbia Law School. She served as director of the ACLU's Women's Rights Project, 1972–1973, and as general counsel from 1973 to 1980.[10]

During her work with the Women's Rights Project, Ginsburg argued five other gender discrimination cases before the Supreme Court. Her success rate was impressive; she won four of the five cases. She was so successful that some legal scholars have referred to her as the "Thurgood Marshall of gender-discrimination law."[11] In the two most well-known cases, *Frontiero v. Richardson* (1973) and *Craig v. Boren* (1976), Ginsburg attempted to convince the Court to analyze gender-based classifications under a higher level of scrutiny than the traditional "rational basis" test. In *Frontiero,* Sharron Frontiero's attorneys allotted Ginsburg ten minutes of their oral argument time so that she could argue for the "strict scrutiny" approach, but she was unable to get a majority of the Court to adopt this standard for gender discrimination cases.

After this failure, Ginsburg shifted her focus and began to suggest that the Court adopt an "intermediate level of scrutiny" for such cases. Her efforts culminated in success in 1976 in *Craig v. Boren,* when a majority announced the "important government objective" test. Under this test, "classifications by gender must serve important governmental objectives and must be substantially related to the achievement of those objectives."[12]

After a decade of Ginsburg's legal advocacy for gender equality, President Jimmy Carter in 1980 appointed her to a judgeship on the prestigious United States Court of Appeals for the District of Columbia Circuit. During her thirteen years on the circuit court, Ginsburg, the legal activist, earned a reputation as a moderate judge. Although her record as a strong legal advocate and a moderate jurist appears contradictory, her colleagues and friends insist that there is no contradiction. They maintain that her records as legal advocate and judge both are characterized by a cautious approach in which the law is changed incrementally. Vivian Berger, Dean of Columbia Law School and Ginsburg's former student, said, "She is a judge's judge and a lawyer's lawyer, meaning she has great regard for the role of judges, which is a conservatizing influence, and a great commitment to issues to which she is committed, such as civil rights and liberties."[13]

Confirmation Politics

By early July, Ginsburg's nomination had been endorsed by key Democratic senators, as well as a few influential Republicans, including Robert Dole of Kansas and Orrin Hatch of Utah. In preparation for the hearings, Ginsburg examined hundreds of her legal briefs, speeches, journal articles, and appellate opinions. In addition, she studied hours of videotapes of the recent hearings. The Senate Judiciary Committee held only four days of hearings on her nomination, beginning July 20. These were the first hearings to be held with a Senate Judiciary Committee that included women among its members. Senators Diane Feinstein of California and Carol Moseley-Braun of Illinois had been elected in 1992 after the backlash from the hearings involving law professor Anita Hill's charges of sexual harassment against Clarence Thomas. The all-white male Judiciary Committee panel was accused of being insensitive to the issue of sexual harassment and of unfair treatment toward Anita Hill during its questioning.

In introducing Ginsburg to the panel, New York Senators Daniel Patrick Moynihan (Democrat) and Alphonse D'Amato (Republican) praised her as a distinguished jurist and offered their unwavering support, as did Eleanor Holmes Norton, the District of Columbia representative to the House of Representatives. Following introductory remarks by the other Judiciary Committee members, Ginsburg set the tone for the hearings with her opening statement. While failed nominee Robert Bork said that serving on the Court would provide an "intellectual feast," she indicated her interest in using her talents to "serve society." She described her judicial philosophy as non-ideological and emphasized that she would approach her work on the Court with careful restraint.

> My approach [to the work of judging] is neither liberal nor conservative. Rather it is rooted in the place of the judiciary, of judges, in our democratic society. . . . The judiciary is third in line and it is placed apart from the political fray. . . .
>
> In Alexander Hamilton's words, the mission of judges is "to secure a steady, upright, and impartial administration of the laws." I would add that the judge should carry out that function without fanfare, but with due care. She should decide the case before her

without reaching out to cover cases not yet seen. She should be ever mindful, as . . . Justice Benjamin Nathan Cardozo said, "Justice is not to be taken by storm. She is to be wooed by slow advances."[14]

In stark contrast to previous nominees Robert Bork and Clarence Thomas, who disavowed most of their written records during their confirmation testimony, Ginsburg requested that committee members "judge my qualifications principally on [my] written record," and she expressed hope that her record would assure them that she was "prepared to do the hard work and to exercise the informed, independent judgment that Supreme Court decisionmaking entails."[15] Most importantly, she then told the Committee that she would not answer questions about issues or cases that might go to the Supreme Court for decision.

> [I]t would be wrong for me to say or to preview in this legislative chamber how I would cast my vote on questions the Supreme Court may be called upon to decide. . . .
>
> Judges in our system are bound to decide concrete cases, not abstract issues. Each case comes to court based on particular facts and its decision should turn on those facts and the governing law. . . . A judge sworn to decide impartially can offer no forecasts, no hints, for that would show not only disregard for the specifics of the particular case, it would display disdain for the entire judicial process.[16]

Not surprisingly, Ginsburg was most animated and comfortable in responding to questions about her personal experiences with gender discrimination and especially with her work on gender equality litigation. She discussed several of the major Supreme Court decisions in this area, including *Reed* and *Frontiero,* and she placed special emphasis on a 1975 case, *Weinberger v. Weisenfeld.*[17] *Weisenfeld* involved a federal regulation that provided for death benefits to a surviving spouse and minor children in the case of a husband's death, but only for the minor children in the event of a wife's death. Ginsburg argued on behalf of Stephen Weisenfeld that this was unconstitutional gender discrimination, and the Court agreed unanimously. This case is an example of Ginsburg's strategy of bringing cases on behalf of male plaintiffs, particularly when the laws being challenged were based on stereotypes of men as breadwinners and women as homemakers. Although she used these types of cases to show how such stereotypes limited women's opportunities, her strategy has been criticized by some women's rights activists.[18] She spoke with pride about *Weisenfeld,* arguing that this case "was the perfect example of how gender-based discrimination hurts everyone."[19]

Ginsburg reaffirmed her support for abortion rights, citing with approval the Court's 1992 decision in *Planned Parenthood v. Casey.*[20] In *Casey,* the Court upheld *Roe v. Wade* although its decision departed from the standards set in that precedent. In *Roe,* the Court had held that abortion was a fundamental right that could be abridged only if the government could prove a compelling interest, and Justice

Blackmun's majority opinion used a framework based on the trimester approach to pregnancy to demonstrate when the government's interests become compelling and to indicate the degree of appropriate government regulation at each stage.[21] *Casey* rejected the trimester framework and held that if a government regulation does not impose an "undue burden" on a pregnant woman's right to abortion, the government need not prove a compelling interest for its policy to be upheld. Some critics of *Casey* contend that as a result of this decision, abortion is no longer a fundamental right. In a brief exchange with Senator Howard Metzenbaum, Ginsburg refused to say whether she agreed with that characterization, stating simply that the ruling in *Casey* affirmed that the abortion right is part of the general right of privacy protected by the liberty clause of the Fourteenth Amendment. She also argued that *Casey* was better than *Roe* in placing the decision in the hands of women because *Roe* focused on the right of the woman along with her consulting physician.

Ginsburg also stood by statements about *Roe* made in her earlier articles and speeches. She told the senators, "My view is that if *Roe* had been less sweeping, people would have accepted it more readily, would have expressed themselves in the political arena in an enduring way on this question. I recognize that this is a matter of speculation."[22] On the question of the legal basis for abortion rights she declared:

> It is essential to woman's equality with man that she be the decisionmaker, that her choice be controlling. If you impose restraints that impede her choice, you are disadvantaging her because of her sex. . . .
> Abortion prohibition by the State . . . controls women and denies them full autonomy and full equality with men. That was the idea I tried to express in the [earlier] lecture. . . . The two strands—equality and autonomy—both figure in the full portrayal.[23]

Perhaps the most contentious periods in the hearings occurred when Senators persisted in asking Ginsburg about her views on the death penalty. Senator Strom Thurmond commented on the length of time involved before an inmate is executed, and he asked whether she agreed that limits should be placed on the post-trial appeals permitted for inmates sentenced to death. She indicated that while finality is important in this type of situation, so is fairness, and she saw the need to balance both principles. When Senator Arlen Specter asked whether she had any scruples against imposing capital punishment, she replied, "My own view of the death penalty . . . is not relevant to any question I would be asked to decide as a judge. I will be scrupulous in applying the law on the basis of the Constitution, legislation, and precedent."[24] Senator Orrin Hatch was even more persistent. He expressed exasperation that she would not simply state her belief on the constitutionality of the death penalty, given her willingness to be specific in discussing abortion, equal rights, and other issues. Ginsburg responded that while she had written and taught about those other issues, "[t]he death penalty is an area that I have never written about."[25]

Despite Committee members' frustration over her unwillingness to answer some of their questions, Ginsburg's confirmation was never in doubt. Her nomination had been endorsed by key senators from both parties even before the hearings began, and the ABA Standing Committee on the Federal Judiciary rated her well qualified by a unanimous vote. On July 29, the Judiciary Committee voted 18–0 to recommend confirmation to the full Senate. On August 3, Judge Ginsburg was confirmed to be a Supreme Court justice by a vote of 96–3, with opposition from Republicans Jesse Helms of North Carolina, Robert Smith of New Hampshire, and Don Nickles of Oklahoma.

Media Coverage and Interest Group Participation

Ginsburg's background and the fact that this was President Clinton's first Supreme Court appointment made this a high-profile nomination, but attention by the print media paled in comparison to coverage of the Bork and Thomas proceedings. Coverage in major national newspapers like the *New York Times, Washington Post,* and *Wall Street Journal* was extensive for the first six days or so after President Clinton announced the nomination but then became more sporadic until a few days before the hearings began. During the period from late June to mid–July, major regional newspapers such as the *Boston Globe, Los Angeles Times, San Francisco Chronicle, Miami Herald, St. Louis Post-Dispatch,* and *Minneapolis Star Tribune* printed a number of feature stories, editorials, and op-ed columns. Predictably, many of the pieces focused on Ginsburg's background as the most prominent litigator in gender discrimination cases and on whether her experience as an advocate for gender equality would influence her Supreme Court performance. Many speculated about her overall impact on the future direction of the Court. Some writers attempted to gauge Ginsburg's positions on various issues by examining key opinions from her service on the federal court of appeals. There was considerable focus on her ideology, with some commentators characterizing her as a moderate and others as a liberal.[26]

As with the nomination of David Souter, the major television networks (ABC, CBS, NBC) did not offer live coverage of Ginsburg's confirmation hearings. PBS provided live, gavel-to-gavel coverage, C-Span offered partial live coverage and then coverage by tape delay, and Court TV provided taped excerpts. CNN covered the press conference announcing Ginsburg's nomination and ABC News Nightline broadcast a special program about a week before the hearings began. Coverage of the nomination and confirmation on the major networks basically was limited to brief stories on their evening news programs.[27]

Considerably fewer interest groups were involved officially in Ginsburg's confirmation hearings than had participated in the previous proceedings. In addition to the ABA Standing Committee on the Federal Judiciary, three organizations testified in favor of confirmation. Representatives of California Women Lawyers, the Hispanic National Bar Association, and the Association of the Bar of the City of New York constituted one panel. The testimony of the Hispanic Bar Asociation representative was especially interesting because he focused on encouraging Ginsburg to be sensitive to the concerns of Hispanics, and, furthermore, he openly advocated for a Hispanic to be appointed to the Court the next time a vacancy arose. This panel had an additional witness, although he did not represent an organization. Stephen Weisenfeld, the litigant represented by Ginsburg in the previously mentioned *Weinberger v. Weisenfeld* case, also strongly recommended that Ginsburg be confirmed.

A second panel was composed of representatives from five organizations urging senators to reject confirmation: Americans United For Life, the March for Life Education and Defense Fund, the Eagle Forum, Family Research Council, and The Conservative Caucus. All but the Eagle Forum focused their remarks on Ginsburg's support of abortion rights. The Eagle Forum's representative encouraged the Judiciary Committee to question Ginsburg carefully about her views on gender and family issues, and this, she said, would demonstrate that the nominee was not a moderate, but an out-of-the-mainstream "radical feminist."

Additional materials for the record were submitted by three other groups: Alliance for Justice, the Judicial Selection Monitoring Project, and the National Asian Pacific American Bar Association. Alliance for Justice is an umbrella organization similar to the Leadership Conference for Civil Rights. This group examined Ginsburg's record both as an advocate and as a judge and expressed hope that she would bring the social justice values from her experience as a legal advocate to her work on the Supreme Court. The Judicial Selection Monitoring Project also examined her record but took issue with the characterization of Ginsburg as a moderate.

Judicial Performance

In her confirmation testimony, Ginsburg identified herself as a moderate, and this self-description generally has proven to be an accurate one. Her first term performance placed her squarely in the middle of the Court, and, although she has shifted to the left much like Souter has, Ginsburg is not a liberal in the tradition of Justices Brennan and Marshall. This section will examine her voting behavior and her positions on various issues, especially those addressed in the confirmation hearings.

Voting Behavior

One study of Ginsburg's initial term on the Court (1993–1994) concluded that she had no single ideological alignment but instead had moderate rates of agreement with all of her colleagues, both conservative and liberal.[28] According to the study's authors, in the Court's nonunanimous cases, she most frequently was aligned with Justices Souter and Kennedy, and to a lesser extent with Justices Stevens and O'Connor. Her interagreement scores with these four justices were 73% (Souter), 69% (Kennedy), 67% (O'Connor), and 64% (Stevens). Her lowest interagreement scores were with the two justices at opposing ends of the ideological spectrum, Blackmun on the left and Thomas on the right. In cases decided by five-member majorities, however, she had the highest agreement with the most liberal justices, Blackmun, Stevens, and Souter. At the same time, Ginsburg joined the majority in a number of cases where these three liberals dissented.

Over time, Ginsburg's voting behavior has moved in a direction similar to that of Justice Souter, so it is not surprising that he is the justice she most often is aligned with. According to the end-of-term statistics in *Harvard Law Review,* for all cases decided with written opinions in the 1995–1996 through 1999–2000 terms, Ginsburg and Souter agreed 84% of the time. Her next highest agreement in that time period was with Justices Breyer (79%) and Stevens (78%), and she agreed least often with Justices Thomas (54%) and Scalia (55%). The Harvard statistical summary of the nonunanimous cases, which the editors began with the 1997–1998 term, illustrates similar patterns. In the three terms from 1997–1998 through 1999–2000, Ginsburg had the highest agreement with Justices Souter (75%), Breyer (66%), and Stevens (64%) and the lowest agreement with Justices Thomas (25%) and Scalia (33%).[29]

Ginsburg's voting behavior in criminal justice cases is especially interesting. In criminal justice cases, a conservative vote favors the government's interest over defendants' claims, and a liberal vote favors the rights of those accused of crimes. Ginsburg began her tenure on the high court as a conservative on criminal justice issues but gradually has become more supportive of liberal outcomes. For example, during the 1995–1996 term, she took a liberal position in less than half of all of the Court's criminal justice decisions (46%) and in slightly more than one-third (36%) of the nonunanimous cases. A term later, the percentages of liberal votes cast by Ginsburg had increased to 53% for all criminal justice cases and 71% for the nonunanimous ones. This increase continued in the next three terms. The percentages of liberal votes for all cases in 1997–1998, 1998–1999, and 1999–2000 were 60%, 68%, and 68%, respectively, while the percentages for the nonunanimous cases were even higher at 68%, 71%, and 77%.[30]

Gender Discrimination

Given Ginsburg's background as a litigator for gender equality, legal experts were particularly interested in how she would decide gender discrimination cases. The wait was brief because the justices heard a sexual harassment case in Ginsburg's first term. In *Harris v. Forklift Systems* (1993), the Court held unanimously that in hostile environment sexual harassment cases brought under Title VII, litigants need not prove psychological injury in order to win monetary damages.[31] Justice O'Connor wrote, "So long as the environment would reasonably be perceived, and is perceived, as hostile or abusive, there is no need for it also to be psychologically injurious."[32] In a brief concurrence Ginsburg emphasized that "[i]t suffices to prove that a reasonable person subjected to the discriminatory conduct would find, as the plaintiff did, that the harassment so altered working conditions as to 'ma[k]e it more difficult to do the job.'"[33] The most interesting part of her concurrence was a footnote regarding the existing standard of review for gender-based classifications in equal protection cases. She wrote, "Indeed, even under the Court's equal protection jurisprudence, which requires 'an exceedingly persuasive justification' for gender-based classifications, it remains an open question whether 'classifications based upon gender are inherently suspect.'"[34] Some analysts wondered whether this footnote was a signal that in some future case Ginsburg would attempt to persuade her colleagues to adopt strict scrutiny for examining gender-based classifications.

Five years after *Harris v. Forklift Systems,* the Court made additional important clarifications to sexual harassment law. Ginsburg joined a unanimous decision holding that same-sex sexual harassment is actionable under Title VII.[35] She also joined seven-member majorities in *Burlington Industries, Inc. v. Ellerth* (1998) and *Faragher v. City of Boca Raton* (1998), ruling that employers may be held liable for the harassing conduct of their supervisors.[36] The Court also held, however, that employers may avoid liability by demonstrating that they "exercised reasonable care to prevent and correct promptly any sexually harassing behavior" and that the employee "unreasonably failed to take advantage of any preventive or corrective opportunities provided by the employer."[37] Conversely, in *Gebser v. Lago Vista Independent School District* (1998), a five-member majority concluded that a school district could not be held financially liable for a teacher's sexual harassment of a student unless the student has informed a school official who has reasonable authority to take action to remedy the problem.[38] In dissent, Ginsburg argued that the standard set by the majority was too high but argued that a district could avoid liability if it can "show that its internal remedies were adequately publicized and likely would have provided redress without exposing the complainant to undue risk, effort, or expense."[39]

Ginsburg wrote the majority opinion in a landmark equal protection case during her third year on the Court. In *United States v. Virginia* (1996), the Court ruled that Virginia Military Institute's exclusively male admissions policy violated the Equal Protection Clause and that the creation of a parallel program at a women's college was not a sufficient remedy. Ginsburg's opinion concluded that VMI's admissions policy was not substantially related to the achievement of an important governmental interest and thereby failed the important government objective test. She said the state's alleged purpose of providing an array of educational options for its students had "afforded a unique educational benefit only to males," and VMI's plan "serves the Commonwealth's sons" but "makes no provision whatever for her daughters."[40] In applying the intermediate standard of review, Ginsburg used the phrases "skeptical scrutiny" and "exceedingly persuasive justification," and, as a result, Justice Scalia strongly attacked her analysis. In a lone dissent, he accused the majority of incorrectly applying intermediate scrutiny and of redefining it in a way "that makes it indistinguishable from strict scrutiny."[41] In an opinion concurring only in the judgment, Chief Justice Rehnquist also noted his concern that the majority opinion's use of the phrase "exceedingly persuasive justification" in connection with intermediate scrutiny introduced confusion to this test.

In her briefs and arguments as an advocate for gender equality, Ginsburg regularly conveyed her belief that gender role stereotypes severely limited women's opportunities to participate fully in every aspect of life. Laws based on these stereotypes, she said, although supposedly passed to provide important benefits to women, actually were quite harmful. In reviewing some landmark gender-discrimination cases during the confirmation hearings, Ginsburg reiterated these concerns. "It was always my view that distinctions on the basis of gender should be treated most skeptically because, historically, virtually every classification that, in fact, limited women's opportunities was regarded as one cast benignly in her favor."[42] It is not surprising, therefore, that in *United States v. Virginia,* Ginsburg focused considerable attention on gender role stereotypes. She asserted that the reasons given for excluding women from VMI were based on outdated and improper stereotypes about the roles and abilities of women. State officials had argued that VMI's adversative method of training students would have to be modified drastically if women were admitted and that this likely would destroy its program. In agreeing with these contentions, the district court accepted findings of the state's expert witnesses regarding "typical tendencies" of men and women. Ginsburg warned:

> [T]he United States emphasizes that time and again since this Court's turning point decision in *Reed v. Reed* (1971), we have cautioned reviewing courts to take a "hard look" at generalizations or "tendencies" of the kind pressed by Virginia, and relied upon by the District Court. State actors controlling gates to opportunity, we have instructed, may not exclude qualified individuals based on "fixed notions concerning the roles and abilities of males and females."

. . . The notion that admission of women would downgrade VMI's stature, destroy the adversarial system and, with it, even the school, is a judgment hardly proved, a prediction hardly different from other "self-fulfilling prophec[ies]" once routinely used to deny rights or opportunities.[43]

In 2001, when the Court upheld a federal policy that requires differential treatment by gender in cases involving out-of-wedlock, foreign-born children of citizen and alien parents, Ginsburg joined Justice O'Connor's strong dissent.[44] O'Connor chastised the majority for sanctioning what she said was a clear equal protection violation and for condoning the stereotype "that mothers must care for these [nonmarital] children and fathers may ignore them."[45]

Abortion Rights

One year before Ginsburg's appointment, the Court affirmed *Roe v. Wade,* holding that the Constitution protects a woman's right to have an abortion. According to the decision in *Planned Parenthood v. Casey* (1992), an abortion regulation is invalid if it poses an "undue burden" on a woman's decision to terminate a pregnancy before fetal viability. Following *Casey,* a number of states passed laws banning so-called "partial birth abortion." Coined by abortion opponents, this non-medical term refers to an abortion procedure used primarily in second-trimester abortions (pre-viability) in which the fetus is aborted after it has been partially delivered.[46] Abortion foes, seeking to erode public support for abortion rights, described it as a particularly cruel and gruesome method of terminating pregnancies.

In *Stenberg v. Carhart* (2000) a deeply fractured Court invalidated Nebraska's ban on partial birth abortions.[47] Writing for the majority, Justice Breyer concluded that the law posed an undue burden on a woman seeking an abortion because it prohibited a procedure that was safer in some circumstances. Moreover, the law did not contain an exception for preserving the health of the mother. While joining Breyer's opinion, Ginsburg issued a brief concurrence. She declared that the law did not "save any fetus from destruction, for it target[ed] only 'a *method* [emphasis in original] of performing abortion'" and that it banned the procedure simply because "State legislators [sought] to chip away at the private choice shielded by *Roe v. Wade*."[48]

Discrimination in Other Areas

At confirmation, Senator Edward Kennedy asked Ginsburg whether her experiences with gender discrimination had made her sensitive to other forms of discrimination. In recalling her childhood experiences of seeing signs such as "No dogs or Jews allowed" displayed prominently in public places, she concluded,

"One couldn't help but be sensitive to discrimination, living as a Jew in America at the time of World War II."[49] Moreover, she noted, "People who have known discrimination are bound to be sympathetic to discrimination encountered by others, because they understand how it feels to be exposed to disadvantageous treatment for reasons that have nothing to do with one's ability, or the contributions one can make to society."[50]

Since joining the Supreme Court, Ginsburg has in fact expressed concern about other forms of discrimination. When a narrow majority limited the authority of federal courts to remedy school segregation in a 1995 ruling, Ginsburg dissented. In *Missouri v. Jenkins*, the Court struck down a district judge's orders that required the state to increase salaries for school personnel and to continue funding for remedial education programs in order to boost the achievement scores of students in the Kansas City Metropolitan School District. Furthermore, the Court declared invalid the magnet school plan that the judge had developed to improve inner-city schools to attract suburban white students in order that the Kansas City schools would be desegregated. Chief Justice Rehnquist's majority opinion said that federal judicial authority in school desegregation cases is limited to remedying the effects of prior *de jure* segregation and that the judge had imposed an "interdistrict remedy" for an "intradistrict violation." Ginsburg joined Justice Souter's dissent, which upheld the authority of the federal court to order the salary increases and the continued funding of remedial programs, and which criticized the majority for ruling on the validity of the magnet school plan. In addition, she wrote a brief separate opinion reviewing the history of state-sponsored segregation in Missouri to illustrate why she believed that the court's desegregation efforts remained necessary. She said that the seven years of remedial programs ordered by the district court paled in comparison to over two centuries of official discrimination practiced against African American students. She concluded, "Today, the Court declares illegitimate the goal of attracting nonminority students to the Kansas City, Missouri School District, and thus stops the District Court's efforts to integrate a school district that was, in the 1984/1985 school year, sorely in need and 68.3% black. Given the deep, inglorious history of segregation in Missouri, to curtail desegregation at this time and in this manner is an action at once too swift and too soon."[51]

Ginsburg's dissent in a 1995 affirmative action decision reflected similar concerns about racial discrimination. In *Adarand Constructors, Inc. v. Pena*, the Court overturned its 1990 holding that federal affirmative action programs would be examined under intermediate scrutiny, while state and local plans would be subjected to strict scrutiny. In *Adarand*, Justice O'Connor's majority opinion stated that strict scrutiny applies to affirmative action programs of all levels of government—federal, state, and local. She maintained, however, that the government is not prohibited from remedying persistent discrimination and its lingering effects, and she insisted that carefully developed affirmative action plans could meet strict scrutiny. In addition to joining dissenting opinions by Justices Stevens and Souter, Ginsburg's dissent (joined by Justice Breyer) emphasized the lingering effects of racial discrimination.

> Those effects, reflective of a system of racial caste only recently ended, are evident in our workplaces, markets, and neighborhoods. Job applicants with identical resumes, qualifications, and interview styles still experience different receptions, depending on their race. White and African-American consumers still encounter different deals. People of color looking for housing still face discriminatory treatment by landlords, real estate agents, and mortgage lenders. Minority entrepreneurs sometimes fail to gain contracts though they are the lowest bidders, and they are sometimes refused work even after winning contracts.[52]

When she was asked in her confirmation hearings about her views regarding discrimination on the basis of sexual orientation, Ginsburg repeatedly refused to give specific answers, simply noting that "rank discrimination" against anyone is deplorable. She said she could not be more specific because a case was very likely to come before the Court for decision. Her prediction was correct. In her third term the Court issued a landmark ruling on this issue. By a 6–3 vote, in *Romer v. Evans* (1996), the Court invalidated a state constitutional amendment prohibiting state and local governments from making policies that protect persons from discrimination on the basis of sexual orientation.[53] Ginsburg joined Justice Kennedy's majority opinion describing the Colorado amendment as furthering arbitrary discrimination against gays and lesbians and therefore contrary to our constitutional tradition. Justice Kennedy concluded, "Amendment 2 classifie[d] homosexuals not to further a proper legislative end but to make them unequal to everyone else. This Colorado cannot do. A State cannot so deem a class of persons a stranger to its laws."[54] By contrast, the dissenters argued that the Colorado Amendment was an attempt to preserve traditional moral values and simply denied homosexuals preferential treatment.

Habeas Corpus and the Death Penalty

On repeated occasions during the hearings, senators asked Ginsburg about her views on capital punishment and reforming the federal habeas process by placing limitations on the post-trial appeals of those sentenced to death. She said that her beliefs about the death penalty were not relevant but that she would apply the law according to the Constitution, legislation, and precedent. Her responses disappointed opponents of capital punishment, who were hoping that she might agree with Justices Brennan and Marshall, who believed the death penalty to be unconstitutional in all circumstances.

Since arriving on the Court, Ginsburg has given no indication that she believes capital punishment to be inherently unconstitutional, but she has taken positions that emphasize providing due process for defendants sentenced to death. During her first term, Ginsburg did not join Justice Blackmun when he announced that he could no longer support the death penalty because he was convinced that it could never be administered fairly. Dissenting from the denial of certiorari in a death penalty case, Blackmun wrote:

> I shall no longer tinker with the machinery of death. For more than 20 years, I have endeavored—indeed, I have struggled—along with the majority of this Court, to develop procedural and substantive rules that would lend more than the mere appearance of fairness to the death penalty endeavor. . . . The problem is that the inevitability of factual, legal, and moral error gives us a system that we know must wrongly kill some defendants, a system that fails to deliver the fair, consistent, and reliable sentences of death required by the Constitution.[55]

In other cases decided at the end of that same term, Ginsburg did not question the constitutionality of the death penalty.

Since 1976, the justices consistently have held that at the sentencing phase of capital cases, juries must consider both aggravating and mitigating circumstances when deciding whether to sentence a defendant to death.[56] In *Simmons v. South Carolina* (1994), a closely divided Court held that in cases where the prosecutor uses the defendant's future dangerousness as an issue in the sentencing phase of a capital trial, and where state law prohibits the defendant's release on parole, the jury must be told of the defendant's parole ineligibility.[57] Here the trial judge refused to provide this information and also directed defense counsel not to divulge it. While Ginsburg joined Justice Blackmun's plurality opinion, she wrote a brief concurrence, stressing that due process requires that defendants have a "right to be heard," which in this case included the opportunity to present a rebuttal argument to the prosecution's claim about his future dangerousness. In *Romano v. Oklahoma* (1994), the Court rejected a defendant's claim that he was entitled to a new sentencing hearing because the prosecution had introduced evidence of his death sentence for an earlier murder.[58] Joined in dissent by Justices Blackmun, Stevens, and Souter, Ginsburg concluded that evidence about the defendant's prior death sentence inappropriately may have influenced the jury's sentencing decision; therefore, he was entitled to a new hearing.

Ginsburg's concerns about balancing finality and fairness are apparent in habeas corpus cases involving death row inmates. For example, in *Gray v. Netherland* (1996), she wrote for the dissenters when a slim majority ruled that a defendant was not entitled to seek federal habeas relief when he alleged that he was not given adequate notice of the prosecution's intent to use certain evidence against him during his sentencing hearing.[59] In Ginsburg's words, "Basic to due process in criminal proceedings is the right to a full, fair, potentially effective opportunity to defend against the State's charges. Petitioner Gray was not accorded that fundamental right at the penalty phase of his trial for capital murder."[60]

Church-State Issues

Conflicts over the Establishment Clause have been some of the most divisive issues in the Court's history. Since the late 1960s, the Court has been divided between justices who support non-preferential government aid to religion—the accommodationist approach—and those who maintain that government may not directly advance or inhibit religion—the neutrality approach. Although she has written very little in this area, Ginsburg appears to support the neutrality approach. For example, in *Board of Kiryas Joel v. Grumet* (1994), she joined a decision invalidating a New York law that created a separate school district for a village of Hasidic Jews in order to provide special education services to their disabled children.[61] One year later, in *Rosenberger v. University of Virginia* (1995), a sharply divided Court held that a public university could provide funds to student groups for religious publications without violating the Establishment Clause.[62] Ginsburg joined Justice Souter's dissent, asserting that the majority had misinterpreted the relevant precedents and the neutrality principle and, in so doing, had approved the government's direct funding of religious activities. In a less visible case decided that same term, Ginsburg wrote her first opinion on church-state issues. *Capital Square Review and Advisory Board v. Pinette* (1995) involved a request by the Ku Klux Klan to place a large cross on the grounds surrounding the Ohio statehouse during the Christmas season. The area previously had been used by a number of groups and individuals, but the review board denied the Klan's request, concluding that placement of the cross on the grounds would violate the Establishment Clause. Seven justices ruled that the request should have been granted, but they had differing reasons for this conclusion.[63] Ginsburg's dissent contended that placement of the cross on the statehouse grounds was an establishment violation because of the absence of a disclaimer indicating that the government did not endorse this expression.

At the end of the 1999–2000 term, in *Santa Fe Independent School District v. Doe* the Court ruled that school-sponsored, student-led prayer at public high school football games violated the Establishment Clause.[64] Ginsburg joined Justice Stevens's majority opinion, which rejected the school district's claim that there was no unconstitutional establishment of religion because the pregame invocations were private speech and students were not coerced into participation. A few weeks later, Ginsburg dissented when a majority held that a federal program which authorizes public funds to be used to provide computers and other equipment to parochial schools did not violate the Establishment Clause.[65] One term later, the justices decided whether a school could refuse to permit a religious group to use its facilities for an after-school bible study and prayer program for elementary school students. In *Good News Club v. Milford Central School* (2001), the Court ruled that because school officials permitted other groups to hold meetings at the school, exclusion of the religious group amounted to viewpoint discrimination in violation of the group's free speech rights.[66] In addition, the majority saw no establishment problem. Ginsburg joined Justice Souter's dissent, which contended that the Good News Club clearly intended to use the school premises "for an evangelical service of worship" and that the Court's decision "stand[s] for the remarkable proposition that any public school opened for civic meetings must be opened for use as a church, synagogue, or mosque."[67]

Judicial Restraint, Consensus-Building, and Collegiality

In her opening statement to the Senate Judiciary Committee, Ginsburg conveyed her commitment to judicial restraint. She said that she understood the role of courts in a democratic society, and she characterized the federal judiciary as "third in line" in our constitutional system and "placed apart from the political fray."[68] She also indicated that a judge should carry out her responsibilities with fairness and impartiality, carefully "decid[ing] the case before her without reaching out to cover cases not yet seen."[69] Later in the hearings, while discussing her belief in striving for collegiality on multiple-judge courts, she stressed the need to decide cases on procedural grounds whenever possible and the importance of consensus building. During her tenure on the high court, she has been diligent about following these principles.

Even when she agrees with the outcome and joins the majority opinion, Ginsburg sometimes writes separately to emphasize the narrowness of the ruling, often to highlight what was not decided in the case. In *Vernonia School District v. Acton* (1995), for example, the Court ruled that there was no Fourth Amendment violation when a school district ordered its student athletes to undergo random drug testing without any suspicion of drug use by these individuals.[70] In a concurring paragraph, Ginsburg stressed that the Court had decided this issue of random drug testing only with respect to student athletes. In her words, "I comprehend the Court's opinion as reserving the question whether the District, on no more than the showing made here, constitutionally could impose routine drug testing not only on those seeking to engage with others in team sports, but on all students required to attend school."[71] *United States v. Alvarez-Sanchez* (1994) involved the safe harbor rule, a federal law permitting federal prosecutors to use a confession made voluntarily within six hours after a defendant has been arrested or detained, but before the individual is brought before a magistrate. This case concerned a defendant who made incriminating statements to federal agents three days after his arrest for state narcotics charges. In a unanimous ruling against the defendant, the

Court declared the safe harbor rule inapplicable to defendants in custody solely on state charges.[72] Ginsburg's concurrence underscored the limitations of the ruling in noting that the Court had not decided "the effect of [the statute] on confessions obtained more than six hours after an arrest on federal charges."[73]

Related to her belief in narrow rulings is her preference for deciding cases on procedural rather than constitutional grounds when possible. *Agostini v. Felton* (1997), an important Establishment Clause decision, is a case in point. In *Agostini,* the Court overturned its previous decision from *Aguilar v. Felton* (1985) concerning parochial aid. The ruling in *Aguilar* had invalidated a New York City practice permitting public school teachers to provide remedial education classes to disadvantaged children in parochial schools under Title I of the Elementary and Secondary Education Act. As a result of this ruling, the classes were moved to public school sites, leased sites, and mobile units near the religious schools, but these arrangements proved to be quite expensive. Subsequently, the city school board and a group of parents filed suit requesting that public school teachers be permitted to offer remedial instruction in the parochial schools. The petitioners claimed that under the Federal Rules of Civil Procedure, their request should be granted because (1) the high cost of compliance with the earlier ruling presented a new factual situation (2) a majority of Rehnquist Court justices had called for *Aguilar* to be overruled, and (3) *Aguilar* had been severely undermined by subsequent Establishment Clause precedents.

Justice O'Connor's majority opinion rejected the first two claims, but she agreed that more recent decisions had in fact undermined *Aguilar* and concluded ultimately that the injunction should be lifted.[74] Ginsburg joined Justice Souter's dissent, which argued that *Aguilar* was correctly decided and was not undermined by subsequent cases, but she also wrote a brief separate opinion focusing on the procedural aspects of the case. In her view, the case should have been decided solely on the basis of the Supreme Court's Rules and the Federal Rules of Civil Procedure, leaving the constitutional issues for a subsequent case. She concluded:

> I find just cause to await the arrival . . . of another case in which our review appropriately may be sought, before deciding whether *Aguilar* should remain the law of the land. That cause lies in the maintenance of integrity in the interpretation of procedural rules, preservation of the responsive, non-agenda-setting character of this Court, and avoidance of invitations to reconsider old cases based on "speculations on chances from changes in" [the Court's membership].[75]

In cases where the justices are in sharp disagreement over the outcome, Ginsburg sometimes writes separately to highlight areas of consensus. In *Adarand,* discussed earlier, the majority ruled that strict scrutiny applies to federal affirmative action programs, not just to those of state and local governments, as the decisions in *Croson* and *Metro Broadcasting* previously had held. Despite the fact that there were multiple opinions in *Adarand*—two concurrences and three dissents—as well as sharp language, Ginsburg declared:

> I write separately to underscore not the differences the several opinions in this case display, but the considerable field of agreement—the common understandings and concerns—revealed in opinions that together speak for a majority of the Court. . . . The divisions in this difficult case should not obscure the Court's recognition of the persistence of racial inequality and a majority's acknowledgment of Congress' authority to act affirmatively, not only to end discrimination, but also to counteract discrimination's lingering effects.[76]

Summary

When President Clinton presented Ruth Bader Ginsburg as his choice to succeed Byron White on the United States Supreme Court, he said that she "cannot be called a liberal or a conservative" because she had "proved herself too thoughtful for such labels."[77] He also described her as a "force for consensus-building" on the high court. His comments were based on the fact that, despite Ginsburg's pioneering efforts as a legal advocate for gender equality, she had gained a reputation on the United States Court of Appeals as a moderate or centrist judge.

Ginsburg's performance on the high court generally has been consistent with President Clinton's description. Although her voting record indicates she is one of the more liberal members of the current Court, she has not shown the kind of liberalism generally associated with Justices Brennan and Marshall. Ginsburg is less prone than were Brennan and Marshall to use the Court and the Constitution to promote social reform. Ginsburg's approach often emphasizes the narrowness of a particular ruling and the need to refrain from deciding a broader issue unnecessary to resolve the case at hand.[78]

Ginsburg has stressed the importance of collegiality on multiple-judge courts. At confirmation, she noted, "It helps in building collegiality if you don't take zealous positions, if you don't write in a overwrought way, if you state your position logically and without undue passion for whatever is the position you are developing."[79] Perhaps the clearest example of her concern for collegiality is the fact that she maintains a very close friendship with Justice Scalia, one of the Court's strongest conservatives and one who is known for his strident, acerbic opinions.

During her confirmation hearings, Ginsburg told the Senate Judiciary Committee that her judicial approach was "neither liberal nor conservative" and that she was prepared "to exercise the informed, independent judgment that Supreme Court decisionmaking entails."[80] From all indications, she has remained true to her word. Ginsburg has earned a reputation as a cautious, moderately liberal justice, well-respected not only by her colleagues but by both liberals and conservatives outside the Court.

CHAPTER FIVE

Stephen Breyer

Pragmatic Moderate

In April of 1994, Justice Harry Blackmun announced his plans to retire at the end of that term. Blackmun, who served on the Court for twenty-four years, underwent a major transformation during his Supreme Court career. During his early years, Blackmun was a conservative. He voted so frequently with Chief Justice Warren Burger, his long-time friend, that he often was referred to as his "Minnesota Twin" or, more derisively, as "hip pocket Harry." Blackmun's authorship of the majority opinion in *Roe v. Wade,* however, marked a turning point. He became increasingly liberal, voting more often with Justices William Brennan and Thurgood Marshall, rather than with Chief Justice Burger. At the time he retired, Blackmun was the most liberal member of the Court.

Blackmun's retirement provided President Clinton the opportunity to make his second appointment to the Court. As with the previous nomination, Clinton was interested in appointing a well-known political figure. He first looked to Senate Majority Leader George Mitchell and Interior Secretary Bruce Babbitt, but both declined for different political reasons. Federal appeals judge Richard Arnold, a friend from Clinton's home state of Arkansas, was not chosen because of health problems. Eventually he turned to Stephen Breyer, another federal appeals court judge who a year earlier had been rumored to be Clinton's choice for the seat that eventually went to Ruth Bader Ginsburg. According to Clinton aides, the President was impressed with Breyer's credentials but did not "connect" with him on a personal level. Critics later pointed out that Breyer was in a physically difficult interview situation. Although in the process of recovering from a serious bicycle accident which left him with a punctured lung and broken ribs, Breyer left his hospital bed in Massachusetts for the meeting with Clinton. In addition to this physical difficulty, there apparently was a public relations problem for the administration in nominating Breyer. Following the interview, stories were leaked about his failure to pay Social Security taxes for a household employee.[1] A year earlier, a similar problem had led to President Clinton's withdrawal of his nomination of Zoe Baird for the position of United States Attorney General.

After several weeks of indecision, on May 13, 1994, Clinton finally announced that Breyer was his choice to succeed Justice Blackmun. Clinton described him as an "outstanding jurist" and consensus builder who has "a clear grasp of the law, a boundless respect for the constitutional and legal rights of the American people, a searching and restless intellect and a remarkable ability to explain complex subjects in understandable terms."[2] Although the announcement was somewhat awkward—Breyer was still in Boston at the time and was not formally introduced to the media until three days later—his nomination was met with praise from both Democratic and Republican senators, including Edward Kennedy and Orrin Hatch, who had both worked with him when he served as counsel to the Senate Judiciary Committee. The general consensus seemed to be that he was a moderate, pragmatic judge who would be confirmed easily and who would make important contributions to the work of the Supreme Court.[3]

Breyer's nomination was not satisfactory to all, however. The harshest critics were representatives of Hispanic organizations who were upset that Clinton did not utilize this vacancy to name the first Hispanic to the Supreme Court. Members of Hispanic communities had been lobbying for several years for the appointment of an Hispanic justice, and supposedly there were Hispanic contenders for this nomination. One representative from the Hispanic National Bar Association charged that Clinton had not given serious consideration to any Hispanics for this seat. He declared, "It's totally unacceptable. It shows his utter disregard for our community."[4] Additional criticism of the nomination came from consumer activists, most notably Ralph Nader, who claimed that Breyer's record was too pro-business. Despite these criticisms, most observers expected a smooth confirmation for Breyer. Indeed, the widespread praise heaped upon Breyer led to this tongue-in-cheek observation by one columnist: "Somebody should be kind and say something cruel about Judge Stephen Breyer. His nomination for the Supreme Court has produced such a blizzard of praise that he must wake in the graveyard stillnesses of 3 A.M. wondering who is out to ruin him. . . . Editorials, columnists and academics blast him with merciless praise."[5]

Stephen Gerald Breyer, like other nominees before him, had very impressive credentials. He was born in San Francisco, California on August 15, 1938. His father was an attorney and administrator in the San Francisco public school system, and his mother was active in local Democratic politics. A product of elite public schools in San Francisco, Breyer enrolled at Stanford University, where he earned his A.B. in philosophy in 1959, graduating with highest honors. Selected as a Marshall Scholar, he received a second bachelor's degree from Magdalen College at Oxford University in 1961. At Oxford, Breyer studied philosophy, politics, and economics and graduated with first class honors. He returned to the United States and entered Harvard Law School, where he became articles editor for the law review and graduated magna cum laude in 1964.[6]

Breyer has worked in various capacities in the judicial, exective, and legislative branches of the national government and as a law professor. From 1964–1965, he served as a law clerk to Supreme Court Justice Arthur Goldberg, most well-known for his concurring opinion in *Griswold v. Connecticut* (1965), the case which established the right of privacy. After his clerkship, Breyer served in the Justice Department as Special Assistant Attorney General for Anti-trust for two years. He left the Justice Department in 1967 to join the faculty at Harvard Law School, where he taught courses in anti-trust law, administrative law, and the regulation of industry until 1980. During this time Breyer held important posts on the staff of the Senate Judiciary Committee, first as special counsel for the Administrative Practices Subcommittee from 1974–1975. In that capacity, he was instrumental in crafting major legislation to deregulate the airline and trucking industries. He was praised by members of both parties for his ability to forge consensus and cooperation among senators in the process of creating complex legislation. The strong bipartisan respect for Breyer continued as a result of his work as chief counsel for the Committee 1979–1980. In addition to these positions, Breyer served as assistant special prosecutor for the Watergate Special Prosecutor Force in 1973 and as an occasional consultant to the Senate Judiciary Committee from 1975–1979.[7]

In 1980, President Jimmy Carter appointed Breyer to a seat on the federal Court of Appeals for the First Circuit, where he served until 1994. He became chief judge of the circuit in 1990. During his service on the First Circuit, Breyer played a key role on the United States Sentencing Commission, a body charged with creating guidelines to provide consistency in sentences for defendants convicted of similar crimes. He has been credited as the primary author of the sentencing guidelines, a complex grid system based on the characteristics of both the defendant and the crime. These guidelines minimize the discretion left to individual judges in sentencing decisions, and, as result, a number of federal judges have criticized them as too rigid.[8] The sentencing guidelines subsequently were upheld by the Supreme Court in 1989.

The Confirmation Hearings

Although the Senate Judiciary Committee held four days of hearings on Breyer's nomination, it was clear from the start that he would be endorsed by the Committee unless some major issue arose. He had strong bipartisan support from the senators, and the ABA Standing Committee on the Federal Judiciary unanimously gave him its highest evaluation. In his opening statement to the Committee, Breyer described his judicial philosophy.

> I believe that the law must work for people. The vast array of Constitution, statutes, rules, regulations, practices and procedures . . . has a single basic purpose. That purpose is to help the many different individuals who make up America—from so many different backgrounds and circumstances, with so many different needs and hopes—its purpose is to help them live together productively, harmoniously, and in freedom.
>
> Keeping that ultimate purpose in mind helps guide a judge through the labyrinth of rules and regulations that the law too often becomes, to reach what is there at bottom, the very human goals that underlie [the] Constitution and the statutes that Congress writes.[9]

What he described to the senators was a pragmatic approach to the law, rather than a single overarching judicial philosophy. Breyer said that judges must focus not only on the impact of court rulings on the individuals involved in a particular case but also on the ruling's effects in other cases. He emphasized that both of these need to be balanced carefully in judicial decision making.

Breyer, like Ruth Bader Ginsburg, indicated his belief in the importance of consensus building and collegiality on appellate courts. He said that consensus serves to reduce the likelihood of subjectivity in judicial decision making by shifting the focus from the egos of individual judges. In addition, because other actors depend upon clear, understandable opinions and rules, consensus helps to provide both clarity and simplicity. In Breyer's view, such consensus is reached not by bargaining, as legislators often do, but by carefully listening and considering other points of view. In language quite similar to Ginsburg's a year earlier, he noted, "You listen to the argument, and even if you say, 'In the opinion, it might be argued that, but we reject that,' the other judge is much happier. The point of view is taken into account, and that tends to draw people together. And then, when the different judges understand that their own ego is less at stake, you do not stick on every little minor thing."[10]

Some of the questions were predictable—controversial civil rights and liberties issues like abortion, capital punishment, affirmative action, and church-state matters—but substantial focus was on economic issues, especially business regulation and antitrust law, Breyer's areas of expertise. A significant portion of the hearings was devoted to a discussion of his academic writings and judicial opinions in these two areas. Less than a year before his nomination, Breyer's controversial book on regulation, *Breaking the Vicious Cycle*,[11] had been published. In this book he was critical of some government regulations, especially those on environmental and health-related matters, arguing that in some cases the costs were prohibitive while the benefits were limited. One example raised by Senator Joseph Biden was a federal appeals court decision reversing an EPA ban on asbestos because the court assumed that since the implementation costs were high, this result could not have been intended under the relevant statute. Biden asked Breyer whether judges should determine congressional intent by considering implementation costs. He responded that he could not say this was never appropriate, but it would depend on what Congress had in mind in the particular statute. In addition, he said that he had written two opposite things about the case in question. On the one hand, he said it was an example of an EPA regulation that was extremely costly but would not save many lives. At the same time, he said it illustrated the importance of judges leaving these kinds of decisions to Congress. The discussion ended with this exchange.

> THE CHAIRMAN. Now, if Congress delegates authority to an agency to consider costs and benefits in implementing the statute, your view is, then, that the Court should, unless there is a clear disregard of that requirement, yield to the agency.

> JUDGE BREYER. Absolutely. [12]

Senator Kennedy asked Breyer how he would respond to claims that he was hostile to health and safety regulations. Breyer explained his view that economics plays a larger role in classical economic regulation, e.g., the trucking and airline industries, and a lesser role in the areas of health, safety, and the environment. He said that in these latter areas "no one would think that economics is going to tell you how much you want to spend helping the life of another person," and this is "a decision for Congress to make reflecting the values of people."[13]

Breyer's anti-trust rulings on the First Circuit were the subject of criticism. Senator Howard Metzenbaum accused him of favoring large corporations over consumers and small business owners, and he cited a law review study which found that Breyer voted against the alleged victims of anti-trust abuse in all sixteen of the cases he had decided. Breyer responded that he did not keep score on the number of victories for plaintiffs and defendants but that he was concerned about making the right decision in each individual case, whether the plaintiff or the defendant was big business. "What I am interested in is is the case correct as a matter of law, and I consider the cases one at a time, and I consider the merits, the legal merits of the arguments in front of me."[14] In responding to Senator Metzenbaum's questions about some specific antitrust rulings, Breyer indicated that in his decisions, he attempted to achieve the purpose of antitrust laws, which is to protect consumers and promote efficient production. His answers were unsatisfactory to Senator Metzenbaum, who said that Breyer's analysis in many cases was too technical and that he hoped he would be more sensitive in antitrust cases to the "little guy" when he joined the Supreme Court.

Despite a few heated exchanges, most of them with Senator Metzenbaum, the hearings were largely undramatic, except for attention to claims that Breyer had mishandled an alleged conflict of interest when he served on the federal court of appeals; this information had been revealed in news stories before the hearings began. Critics suggested that Breyer should have recused himself from eight environmental pollution cases because he held an investment in Lloyd's of London, an insurance firm that stood to lose major sums of money from such lawsuits. After discovering that this could be a major point of contention, Breyer attempted to attack this issue head-on, at the end of his opening statement to the Committee. He said that he had studied the cases and the judicial recusal statute and was certain that he had not violated any ethical standards by participating in these cases. However, he said he recognized the problem presented by even the appearance of a conflict of interest and therefore would seek to dissolve the investments and the relationship with Lloyd's. Despite Breyer's attempt to ward off attention from this issue, committee members questioned him repeatedly about it. Breyer insisted that he had done nothing that was unethical and that he would take extra care in avoiding similar problems in the future.

In keeping with the policy established after the public spectacle of the second round of the Clarence Thomas hearings, on the morning of Breyer's final appearance before the Committee, members went into closed session to consider any concerns that should not be raised publicly. Senator Biden reported that nothing significant came out of this closed session. Questions already had been raised regarding the alleged conflict of interest from Breyer's Lloyd's of London investment. In addition, on the last day of his public appearance, Breyer responded to specific questions about the "Zoe Baird" problem. Breyer explained that the problem was related to whether the worker is classified as an independent contractor; if so, no Social Security taxes are required. If the employee is not classified as such, employers are obligated to pay the taxes. The problem arose because the Breyers' housekeeper lost her independent contractor status, but, because they did not know this, the requisite taxes were not paid for a couple of years. Subsequently, however, they began to pay the taxes and were assessed a penalty from the IRS, but that penalty later was revoked when the IRS determined that they had acted in good faith.[15]

Although Breyer's alleged conflict of interest attracted considerable attention during the hearings (and the later floor debate), it was not serious enough to derail his nomination. On July 19, four days after the hearings ended, the Judiciary Committee voted unanimously to recommend his confirmation by the full Senate. Ten days later, he was confirmed by a vote of 87–9, with opposition only from Republican senators, most of them conservatives.

Media Coverage and Interest Group Particpation

Breyer's nomination and confirmation proceedings were not covered as extensively by the print media as was the Thomas appointment and, to a lesser extent, the Souter and Ginsburg nominations. This is not surprising because his was not a pivotal appointment in terms of shifting the ideological balance on the Court. Nor was this nomination historic or high-profile, like that of Ruth Bader Ginsburg, who had built a reputation as the leading legal advocate for gender equality and women's rights. In addition, media interest likely was lower because Breyer enjoyed bipartisan support and was not likely to face much opposition in the Senate.

After the nomination was announced on May 13, the *New York Times, Washington Post,* and *Wall Street Journal* covered it fairly extensively for the first few days but gave it only sporadic attention from late May until shortly before the hearings began on July 10. During this period, a number of feature stories, columns, and editorials appeared in major regional newspapers, including the *Boston Globe, Los Angeles Times, St. Louis Post-Dispatch, The Baltimore Sun, Minneapolis Star-Tribune,* and the *Miami Herald.* Many of the stories and commentaries in both the national and regional publications discussed his background as legal counsel for the Senate Judiciary Committee and as a federal judge, emphasizing that he was respected in both arenas as a moderate, pragmatic consensus builder. The minimal level of controversy over Breyer's appointment was another prominent theme. Some writers focused on his financial status and on the alleged conflict of interest described in the previous section of this chapter. Ironically, several of the early stories did not focus directly on Breyer but on Clinton's handling of the process and his decision to appoint Breyer instead of Interior Secretary Bruce Babbitt or federal appeals judge Richard Arnold. In keeping with its previous practice, the *New York Times* provided daily excerpts of the confirmation proceedings.[16]

With respect to the broadcast media, Breyer's confirmation hearings were televised by PBS, C-Span, and Court TV. As might be expected, there was no television coverage by the major networks (ABC, CBS, NBC). CNN provided live coverage of the nomination announcement, but ABC News Nightline did not do a special feature on the first day of the confirmation hearings as it had done for the Souter and Ginsburg proceedings.[17]

The pattern of interest group participation in the Breyer hearings was similar to that for Ginsburg the previous year. That is, the number of groups testifying before the Committee was markedly lower than in the Bork, Thomas, and Souter confirmation hearings. First, a panel representing the ABA Standing Committee on the Federal Judiciary reported that Breyer had received the organization's highest rating, well qualified, by a unanimous vote. Most of the testimony in favor of confirmation came not from interest group representatives but from individuals, including law professors and other prominent attorneys. The Association of the Bar of the City of New York was the only organization to testify in support of confirmation.

Opposition came from Americans United for Life (abortion), the Home School Legal Defense Association (free exercise concerns), and Public Citizen's

Health Research Group (occupational and environmental health and food safety issues). Representatives from various organizations representing attorneys of color testified as well, not to support or oppose confirmation, but to stress their concerns that appointees to the high court should be sensitive to civil rights issues. These groups included the National Bar Association, Coalition of Bar Associations of Color, Hispanic Bar Association, National Asian-Pacific Bar Association, and Native American Bar Association.

Judicial Performance

Based on his reputation and performance on the federal court of appeals, most legal experts predicted that Breyer would be a moderately liberal justice on the high court. Civil libertarians and civil rights activists were especially curious about his position on civil rights and liberties issues because he did not have much of a record in these areas. His expertise was primarily in economic regulation and antitrust law. Breyer has, however, written opinions in important civil rights and liberties cases, including abortion, church-state matters, the First Amendment, and electoral redistricting. He is most well-known perhaps for his opinions in cases involving federalism and the congressional regulation of commerce.

Voting Behavior

Breyer has had a moderately liberal voting record since his initial term on the Court, 1994–1995. According to one study, during that term he had moderate agreement rates in nonunanimous decisions with every justice, from a low of 42.6% with Justice Clarence Thomas, to a high of 78.7% with Justice Ruth Bader Ginsburg. He clearly was not an extreme liberal as conservative opponents predicted; his interagreement score with Justice John Paul Stevens, the most liberal justice, was only 59.6%, compared to his higher scores with two of the conservative justices, Anthony Kennedy (63.8%) and Sandra Day O'Connor (68.1%). Breyer's highest agreement rates were with Justices Ginsburg (78.7%) and David Souter (76.6%), widely viewed as moderate-liberals. The liberal aspect of Breyer's voting record in the 1994–1995 term is seen most clearly in the decisions where the justices were sharply divided. In the Court's sixteen 5–4 decisions, he was a member of the liberal bloc that included Justices Stevens, Ginsburg, and Souter.[18]

Harvard Law Review's annual statistical summaries of the Court's term provides additional evidence of Breyer's moderately liberal voting record. For all cases decided during the 1995–1996 through 1999–2000 terms, his highest levels of agreement were with Justices Souter (82%) and Ginsburg (79%). He agreed least often with Justices Thomas (53%) and Scalia (54%). Breyer also had high levels of agreement with the most liberal justice (Stevens) at 75% and with a moderate-conservative (O'Connor) at 72%. The *Harvard Law Review* statistics show similar results for nonunanimous cases decided during the 1997–1998 through 1999–2000 terms. Breyer agreed most often with Justices Souter and Ginsburg at 69% and 66%, respectively, and his lowest levels of agreement were with Justices Scalia (27%) and Thomas (28%).[19]

Data from several studies on the Court's criminal justice decisions provide further evidence of Breyer's moderate liberalism. In all criminal justice cases decided in the five terms from 1995–1996 through 1999–2000, he took a liberal position in support of defendants' claims only about half the time (50%, 57%, 51%, 45%, and 55%). In nonunanimous cases, his scores fluctuated rather dramatically. During the 1995–1996 term, he supported a liberal outcome in 46% of the cases, but in the next term his liberalism increased significantly to 77%. Breyer supported defendants' claims in 64% of the cases in 1997–1998, but his liberalism score dropped sharply in 1998–1999 to 36%, and increased again to 59% in 1999–2000. Interestingly, the 36% liberalism score in 1998–1999 was the same as Justice Scalia's, one of the Court's most conservative members.[20]

Abortion

Predictably, abortion was an important topic of discussion during Breyer's confirmation hearings. After all, he was to succeed Justice Blackmun, author of the majority opinion in *Roe* and the strongest supporter of abortion rights on the Court. Furthermore, the 5–4 vote in the 1992 *Planned Parenthood v. Casey* decision affirming a woman's right to an abortion before viability of the fetus, demonstrated the tenuous nature of this constitutional right. Indeed, Justice Blackmun noted this in his concurrence. After praising the trio of Justices Souter, O'Connor, and Kennedy for what he termed their act of courage, Blackmun concluded,

> In one sense, the Court's approach is worlds apart from that of the Chief Justice and Justice Scalia [strong dissenters in *Casey*]. And yet, in another sense, the distance between the two approaches is short—the distance is but a single vote.
>
> I am 83 years old, I cannot remain on this Court forever, and when I do step down, the confirmation process for my successor well may focus on the issue before us today. That, I regret, may be exactly where the choice between the two worlds will be made.[21]

As a federal appeals court judge, Breyer had participated in only two cases involving abortion. In one case, he voted to strike down the so-called "gag rule," a federal regulation prohibiting family planning clinics that received federal funds from providing abortion counseling. The Supreme Court subsequently upheld the gag rule in its controversial decision in *Rust v. Sullivan* (1991).[22] In the other case, he voted to deny a challenge to a law requiring parental notification for minors seeking abortions on the grounds that the law was consistent with Supreme Court precedent. Given this limited record, Senators asked Breyer about his views on *Roe v. Wade* and more specifically about whether he agreed with its holding that the state could not prohibit abortion during the first trimester of pregnancy. He said that *Roe* was settled law and that it had been affirmed in *Planned Parenthood v. Casey*, but he would not answer questions regarding the application of the right to abortion because of the possibility of further Supreme Court cases on this issue.

Given the unconstitutionality of laws prohibiting abortion before viability, a number of states have sought to find other ways to restrict abortions. One method used is the enactment of statutes prohibiting so-called partial birth abortions, a procedure used primarily in second-trimester abortions (before viability) in which the fetus is aborted after it has been partially delivered.[23] A number of states have adopted such laws, but federal legislation was vetoed by President Clinton. Many of these statutes have been challenged in federal court, and different rulings by the federal circuits ensured that the issue would have to be addressed by the Supreme Court.

During the 1999–2000 term, the justices heard a case from Nebraska involving a challenge to that state's ban on partial birth abortion. Nebraska law prohibits these abortions from being performed unless necessary to save the life of the woman and defines partial birth abortion as a procedure in which the doctor "partially delivers vaginally a living unborn child before killing the . . . child." The statute indicates that the latter phrase means "intentionally delivering into the vagina a living unborn child, or a substantial portion thereof, for the purpose of performing a procedure that the [doctor] knows will kill the . . . child and does kill the . . . child." Physicians accused of violating this statute are charged with a felony, and conviction results in the automatic loss of a state license to practice medicine. By a 5–4 vote, with Justice Breyer writing the majority opinion, the Court struck down the Nebraska law.[24] Breyer first affirmed that *Casey* and *Roe* were settled law and that these two cases strongly reaffirmed a woman's right to choose an abortion during the early stages of pregnancy. His majority opinion focused on the language in the statute as well as medical information about various abortion procedures. He concluded that the law was invalid because it did not provide an exception for preserving the health of the woman as required by *Casey*. In addition, the statute failed *Casey* because it imposed an undue burden on a woman's right to choose an abortion.[25]

Chief Justice Rehnquist and Justices Scalia, Kennedy, and Thomas filed bitter dissents. Kennedy's dissent was especially significant because he had been a member of the trio in *Casey* that was ultimately responsible for upholding *Roe* and thus affirming a woman's right to choose.

Church-State Issues

The Rehnquist Court has been deeply divided over the proper approach to use in deciding Establishment Clause disputes. The most conservative justices, Rehnquist, Scalia, and Thomas, are advocates of government accommodation, in which government support for religion is permitted as long as the government does not show favoritism towards particular religious groups. By contrast, Justices Stevens, Souter, and Ginsburg, the liberals, adhere to government neutrality, which requires that government may neither advance nor inhibit religion. Justices O'Connor and Kennedy, the Court's moderate-conservatives, have adopted somewhat of a middle position—supporting accommodation sometimes and neutrality at other times. Breyer's position seems to be somewhere between the Stevens-Souter-Ginsburg bloc and Justice O'Connor's middle position.

In *Rosenberger v. University of Virginia* (1995), Breyer dissented when a five-member majority held that the university could not exclude a student group's religious publications from funding provided to other nonreligious student groups.[26] He joined Justice Souter's lengthy dissent chiding the majority for misinterpreting relevant precedents and for "approv[ing] direct funding of core religious activities by an arm of the State."[27] Similarly, in *Santa Fe Independent School District v. Doe* (2000), Breyer joined Justice Stevens's majority opinion invalidating a school policy permitting organized, student-led prayer at public high school football games. Justice Stevens wrote, "The delivery of a message such as the invocation here—on school property, at school-sponsored events, over the school's public address system, by a speaker representing the student body, under the supervision of school faculty, and pursuant to a school policy that explicitly and implicitly encourages public prayer—is not properly characterized as 'private' speech."[28] Chief Justice Rehnquist's strongly worded dissent, joined by Justices Scalia, Kennedy, and Thomas, accused the majority of outright hostility toward religion.

That same term, Breyer took a more conservative position in a case concerning the use of public funds to buy computers and other instructional materials for religious schools. In *Mitchell v. Helms* (2000), by a 6–3 vote, the Court held that this did not create an unconstitutional establishment of religion, but there was no majority opinion.[29] Justice Thomas's plurality opinion contended that the policy was not prohibited because the assistance was provided in a neutral and nondiscriminatory manner to both religious and nonreligious schools. Moreover, the plurality saw no constitutional problem even if the aid was later diverted to religious purposes. Breyer joined Justice O'Connor's opinion, concurring in the judgment only, wherein she rejected the plurality's interpretation of neutrality with respect to programs that provide government funding to a variety of groups, including religious organizations. According to Justice O'Connor, the plurality's analysis of neutrality came close to recognizing it as the single most important factor for deciding future school-aid programs challenged on establishment grounds. Although conceding that neutrality is an important factor, Justice O'Connor said that the Court has "never held that a government-aid program passes constitutional muster *solely* because of the neutral criteria it employs as a basis for distributing aid."[30] In addition, she took issue with the plurality's approval of using this type of government aid for religious purposes. Such a practice, according to Justice O'Connor, was neither consistent with the Court's precedents nor constitutionally permissible.

A year later, Breyer voted with the conservatives when the Court held that a public school could not refuse to allow a religious group to use its building for an after school program involving bible study and prayer for elementary school students. Justice Thomas's majority opinion in *Good News Club v. Milford Central School* (2001) said that by permitting other groups to hold meetings, the school had violated the club's free speech rights by engaging in viewpoint discrimination.[31] Thomas also concluded that the school would not violate the Establishment Clause by allowing this group to meet there. Breyer wrote a partial concurrence endorsing the outcome and part of the opinion but offered several observations regarding the conclusion that there would be no establishment problem in allowing the group to use the school's facilities. He emphasized that government neutrality is only one consideration relevant to deciding establishment violations in this type of situation and that a major concern is whether the school policy has an endorsement effect. "[T]he critical Establishment Clause question here may well prove to be whether a child, participating in the Good News Club's activities, could reasonably perceive the school's permission for the club to use its facilities as an endorsement of religion."[32] Breyer's opinion relied to a large degree on statements from Justice O'Connor's previous opinions.

Cable Television, the Internet, and Political Speech

In recent years, changing technology has required the high court to examine policies regulating cable television and the Internet. Although the justices had earlier ruled that different types of media (print and broadcast) could, consistent with the First Amendment, be treated differently, these new technologies brought new challenges. Some have called for greater regulations on cable television operators and the Internet to protect children from being exposed to sexually oriented materials. Opponents of such policies view them as inappropriate government censorship. During his confirmation hearings, Breyer was asked about the government's authority to protect children from explicit materials, and he simply noted that precedents did allow for differential treatment of different types of media, and there were still many disagreements about this. Along with his colleagues, he has struggled to determine the appropriate scope of regulation.

Denver Area Educational Telecommunications Consortium v. Federal Communications Commission (1996) involved a challenge to three sections of a federal law that attempted to regulate "patently offensive" materials on cable TV.[33] The Court declared two of the three sections unconstitutional, while the other was held to be a valid regulation. Breyer's plurality opinion emphasized the difficulty of this issue, and he cautioned his colleagues to avoid trying to use a categorical approach for a changing area of technology. He said that the appropriate precedent was the 1978 *Federal Communications Commission v. Pacifica Foundation* case, which permitted the government to prohibit the use of certain indecent words over the radio in order to protect children. In Breyer's view, while the first provision was consistent with the First Amendment, the second and third provisions were not because they "[we]re not appropriately tailored to achieve the basic, legitimate objective of protecting children from exposure to 'patently offensive' material."[34] He concluded that these regulations were too restrictive and risked infringing on protected speech.

Only a year after the *Denver* case, the first case involving regulation of sexual communications over the Internet made it on to the Court's agenda. The Communications Decency Act of 1996 contained two controversial provisions: (1) an indecency provision prohibiting the knowing transmission of indecent messages to persons under 18 years old and providing criminal penalties for violators, and (2) a provision sanctioning criminal penalties against anyone who knowingly communicates "in terms patently offensive as measured by contemporary community standards, sexual or excretory activities or organs." In *Reno v. ACLU* (1997), by a 7–2 vote, the Court struck down both of these provisions on the grounds that they were vague, overbroad, and not narrowly tailored to achieve the goal of protecting children from harmful material.[35] Concern that the law threatened to chill protected speech was reflected in Justice Stevens's majority opinion which Breyer joined.

While he believed that the government regulations challenged in *Denver* and *Reno v. ACLU* went too far, Breyer reached the opposite conclusion in *United States v. Playboy Entertainment Group, Inc.*, decided in the 1999–2000 term.[36] At issue was a federal law requiring cable television systems to limit sexually explicit channels to late-night hours. A five-member majority led by Justice Kennedy struck down the law as a violation of the First Amendment. Breyer issued a strong dissent, defending the law as the only effective means to achieve the government's compelling interest in protecting children from sexually explicit programming. He said that while the law may have made it less convenient for adults to watch such programs, it did not prohibit adult speech. In concluding, Breyer wrote:

> Congress has taken seriously the importance of maintaining adult access to the sexually explicit channels here at issue. It has tailored the restrictions to minimize their impact upon adults while offering parents help in keeping unwanted transmissions from their

children. By finding "adequate alternatives" where there are none, the Court reduces Congress' protective power to the vanishing point. That is not what the First Amendment demands.[37]

Breyer testified before the Judiciary Committee that he held political speech and speech related to science, art, and literature at the core of First Amendment protection. The Court has decided several cases involving political speech since he arrived. In *Colorado Republican Federal Campaign Committee v. Federal Election Commission* (1996), the Court voted 7–2 to overturn a Federal Election Commission ruling that the state Republican Party's use of campaign expenditures for radio ads attacking the Democratic senatorial candidate was a violation of federal election expenditure rules.[38] The Democratic Party had argued that the ad expenditures were illegal because the state party already had given the maximum amount of funds to the National Republican Senatorial Committee. Breyer wrote a three-person plurality opinion holding that the party's spending was not a violation of federal election expenditure rules, based on the distinction made in *Buckley v. Valeo* (1976) between financial contributions to a campaign and independent expenditures on a campaign. He concluded that "restrictions on independent expenditures significantly impair the ability of individuals and groups to engage in direct political advocacy and represent substantial . . . restraints on the quantity and diversity of political speech."[39]

In the 1999–2000 term, the Court heard a challenge to a state law regarding campaign funding. At issue in *Nixon v. Shrink Missouri Government PAC* (2000) was a state law limiting campaign contributions to $1,000, the same as permitted under federal campaign law. Commentators had speculated that this case might be used to overturn the longstanding *Buckley* precedent, but the Court affirmed that decision in upholding the Missouri campaign limit. Breyer joined the majority opinion, but he also wrote a separate concurrence emphasizing his belief that the decision did not weaken the First Amendment, as the dissenters had claimed. His position was that limits of this nature actually strengthen the First Amendment and the protection of political speech.

> [R]estrictions upon the amount any one individual can contribute to a particular candidate seek to protect the integrity of the electoral process— the means through which a free society democratically translates political speech into concrete governmental action. . . . Moreover, by limiting the size of the largest contributions, such restrictions aim to democratize the influence that money itself may bring to bear upon the electoral process. In doing so, they seek to build public confidence in that process and broaden the base of a candidate's meaningful financial support, encouraging the public participation and open discussion that the First Amendment itself presupposes.[40]

Not surprisingly, then, in the following year he joined the majority in upholding federal limits on the amount that political parties can spend in coordination with a political candidate in *FEC v. Colorado Republican Federal Campaign Committee* (2001).[41]

Civil Rights

While Breyer has written very few opinions regarding claims of discrimination and the scope of remedies appropriate to address discrimination, this is one of the areas where he is most liberal. With respect to race, he has voted in favor of affirmative action and has supported broad federal judicial authority to remedy school segregation. In addition, he has joined rulings that struck down a state military college's exclusively-male admissions policy and that invalidated a state law preventing governments from banning policies that discriminate on the basis of sexual orientation.

One civil rights area where Breyer has written opinions is redistricting, specifically the validity of so-called majority-minority districts. One year before he was appointed to the high court, the justices ruled 5–4 in *Shaw v. Reno* (1993) that a redistricting plan which resulted in the creation of two majority-black congressional districts in North Carolina could be challenged by white voters as a violation of their right to equal protection.[42] Moreover, the majority held that such plans would be examined using the "strict scrutiny" standard. Under this standard, the plans could be upheld only if they were narrowly tailored to achieve a compelling interest. This ruling spawned additional litigation challenging majority-minority congressional districts in other states, and it continued the North Carolina lawsuit. In Breyer's first term, a five-member majority in *Miller v. Johnson* (1995) invalidated Georgia's plan on the grounds that race was the predominant factor in drawing the district lines and that the state had not demonstrated that the plan was narrowly tailored to achieve a compelling interest in remedying past discrimination.[43] Breyer joined Justice Ginsburg's dissent, which concluded that race was not the predominant factor in designing the districts, but that traditional non-racial districting factors, including protection of an incumbent's seat, were the reasons for the design. Justice Ginsburg also warned the majority that its decision likely would increase federal judicial intervention into state redistricting decisions. A year later, Breyer dissented from two decisions, *Shaw v. Hunt* (a follow-up to 1993 case) and *Bush v. Vera*, which invalidated four majority-minority districts in North Carolina and Texas—three majority-black and one majority-Hispanic.[44] He joined dissents by Justices Stevens and Souter criticizing the majority's application of strict scrutiny in striking down these plans. In *Abrams v. Johnson* (1997), the follow-up to the 1995 *Miller* decision, the Court invalidated a plan by the Georgia legislature that created two majority-black districts, concluding that the second district was the result of an improper racial gerrymander rather than traditional, neutral districting principles.[45] In a dissenting opinion joined by Justices Stevens, Souter, and Ginsburg,

Breyer asserted that the Court should have respected the preference of the Georgia legislature, which was responding to the state's long history of race discrimination in voting. He concluded, "The Court, perhaps by focusing upon what it considered to be unreasonably pervasive positive use of race as a redistricting factor, has created a legal doctrine that will unreasonably restrict legislators' use of race, even for the most benign, or antidiscriminatory purposes."[46]

In the 2000–2001 term, Breyer wrote the majority opinion in another important redistricting case involving the same North Carolina district that had been challenged in the 1993 and 1996 *Shaw* cases. After the state legislature had reconfigured the district, a lower federal court again ruled that the district resulted from inappropriate considerations of race. Breyer's opinion in *Hunt v. Cromartie* (2001) held that race was one of the legislature's considerations but that it was not the dominant factor.[47] After carefully reviewing the evidence considered by the lower court, he concluded that when racial identification is strongly correlated with party affiliation, majority-minority districts are not necessarily evidence of unconstitutional racial gerrymandering. The 5–4 ruling in this case was determined by Justice O'Connor's vote. This was especially significant because it was her majority opinion in the initial *Shaw* case that placed the Court in the middle of redistricting disputes. The new decision is viewed as providing critical guidance to lower court judges responsible for deciding these disputes.

Commerce Power and Federalism

While Breyer has not written many opinions in cases concerning the most "hot-button" civil liberties and civil rights issues, he has been much more vocal in significant contemporary disputes about the scope of congressional authority under the Commerce Clause and conflicts over federalism. The Court has been divided into two blocs on these issues—Chief Justice Rehnquist and Justices Scalia, Thomas, Kennedy, and O'Connor on one side, with Justices Stevens, Souter, Ginsburg, and Breyer on the other.

In his first term, Breyer wrote the lead dissent in a landmark ruling that struck down a congressional exercise of the commerce power. Except for a 1976 ruling, this was the first time in several decades that the Court invalidated a policy enacted by Congress under its authority to regulate commerce. In *United States v. Lopez* (1995), a five-member majority held the Gun Free School Zones Act of 1990 unconstitutional.[48] Chief Justice Rehnquist said that the relevant commerce power precedents required the Court to determine whether the activity being regulated—possession of firearms in a school zone-"substantially affected" interstate commerce. The government's claim that interstate commerce was substantially affected because guns in and around schools could lead to violent crime, which negatively affects the national economy, did not persuade Chief Justice

Rehnquist. By contrast, Breyer, joined by Justices Stevens, Souter, and Ginsburg, accepted the government's claims. He wrote, "[T]he evidence of (1) the extent of the gun-related violence problem (2) the extent of the resulting negative effect on classroom learning, and (3) the extent of the consequent negative commercial effects, when taken together, indicate a threat to trade and commerce that is 'substantial.'"[49] He also asserted that the majority's decision was inconsistent with the Court's modern Commerce Clause precedents and that its attempt to distinguish between "commercial" and "noncommercial" transactions, when each has an identical effect on interstate commerce, was misplaced.

Breyer also dissented in an important commerce power case from the 1999–2000 term. By a 5–4 vote, the Court ruled in *United States v. Morrison* (2000) that the civil damages provision of the Violence Against Women Act (VAWA) was beyond Congress's regulatory authority. This provision of VAWA provided for victims of gender-motivated violence to file suits against their attackers in federal court. Relying to a large extent on *Lopez,* Chief Justice Rehnquist concluded that violence against women did not constitute an economic activity nor was it substantially related to interstate commerce. "We . . . reject the argument that Congress may regulate noneconomic, violent criminal conduct based solely on that conduct's aggregate effect on interstate commerce."[50] The majority rejected extensive findings by Congress demonstrating the effects of violence against women on interstate commerce. In addition to joining Justice Souter's dissent, which was especially critical of the majority's refusal to accept the congressional findings, Breyer wrote separately to emphasize the difficulty of applying the standard set by the majority for determining appropriate limits on federal commerce power. According to Breyer, "The 'economic/noneconomic' distinction is not easy to apply. Does the local street corner mugger engage in 'economic' activity or 'noneconomic' activity when he mugs for money? . . . Would evidence that desire for economic domination underlies many brutal crimes against women save the present statute? The line becomes yet harder to draw given the need for exceptions."[51]

Federalism is another area where Breyer has been aligned with the liberals, usually in dissent. In *Printz v. United States* (1997), the Court struck down a portion of the 1993 Brady Handgun Violence Prevention Act. The Brady Act required the creation of a national database for instant background checks for potential gun purchasers, but in the meantime, local chief law enforcement officers were to conduct these background checks and file written reports in their respective states. A five-member majority led by Justice Scalia held that the federal government could not order state or local law enforcement officers to carry out these functions. According to Justice Scalia, "The Federal Government may neither issue directives requiring the States to address particular problems, nor command the State's officers, or those of their political subdivisions, to administer or enforce a federal regulatory program. . . .[S]uch commands are fundamentally incompatible with our constitutional system of dual sovereignty."[52] This "dual sovereignty" interpretation of federalism is one that had been rejected by the Court over a decade earlier. In addition to joining Justice Stevens's dissent which rejected Justice Scalia's dual sovereignty approach, Breyer wrote a brief dissent. He said that the Court could find guidance on this question in the "comparative experience" of other federal systems, specifically Switzerland, Germany, and the European Union. That experience, Breyer noted, suggests that "there is no need to interpret the Constitution as containing an absolute principle—forbidding the assignment of virtually any federal duty to any state official."[53]

The *Printz* ruling generated a great deal of speculation that the Court was embarking on a major revision of its federalism jurisprudence. Additional decisions have continued the trend toward limiting federal authority that was established in *Printz*. For example, in *Alden v. Maine* (1999), the same five-member majority ruled that state employees cannot file suits in their state courts for violations of the Fair Labor Standards Act (FLSA).[54] Congress had provided in the FLSA for state employees to bring suits for violations in federal or state courts. Because an earlier decision, *Seminole Tribe v. Florida* (1996),[55] held that Congress cannot abrogate state's sovereign immunity from suits in federal courts, the Maine employees brought a suit in state court. The majority ruled in *Alden,* however, that the same principle applied in state courts. Breyer joined Justice Souter's dissent challenging the majority's dual sovereignty interpretation of federalism and noting the practical effects of the decision. Souter noted that as a result of the *Seminole Tribe* and *Alden* decisions, state employees had no real remedies for violations of the FLSA, given that suits for enforcement of the Act were prevented in both state and federal courts.

Two years after *Alden,* in a similar case, *Board of Trustees of the University of Alabama v. Garrett* (2001), the Court held that state employees may not sue their states for damages for violations of the Americans with Disabilities Act (ADA). Chief Justice Rehnquist wrote, "[I]n order to authorize private individuals to recover money damages against the States, there must be a pattern of discrimination by the states which violates the Fourteenth Amendment, and the remedy imposed by Congress must be congruent and proportional to the targeted violation. Those requirements are not met here."[56] Rehnquist said that Congress had not provided sufficient evidence that states historically have discriminated against individuals with disabilities. Breyer took issue with Rehnquist's conclusions in his opinion for the four dissenters. He pointed to congressional hearings and to the work of a special task force convened by Congress to consider the problem of discrimination against people with disabilities.

> The powerful evidence of discriminatory treatment throughout society in general, including discrimination by private persons and local governments, implicates state governments as well, for state agencies form part of that same larger society. . . . There are

roughly 300 examples of discrimination by state governments themselves in the legislative record. I fail to see how this evidence "falls far short of even suggesting [a] pattern of unconstitutional discrimination."[57]

Judicial Philosophy

When President Clinton nominated Stephen Breyer to the high court, he was described by senators, colleagues, and many in the legal community as a pragmatist. Breyer's appearance before the Senate Judiciary Committee bolstered this image. In his opening statement he noted:

> [W]hat you worry about is someone trying to decide an individual case without thinking out the effect of that decision on a lot of other cases. That is why I always think law requires both a heart and a head. If you do not have a heart, it becomes a sterile set of rules, removed from human problems, and it will not help. If you do not have a head, there is the risk that in trying to decide a particular person's problem in a case that may be fine for that person, you cause trouble for a lot of other people, making their lives yet worse.[58]

He expressed similar sentiments when Senator Orrin Hatch asked how a justice should decide constitutional questions in situations where the relevant constitutional provision is unclear. "[Y]ou look to precedent, and you look to tradition, and you look to history if the case is really difficult. And you have to have some understanding of the practical facts of how people live."[59]

As evidenced from his testimony and judicial performance, Breyer does not appear to have an overarching judicial philosophy that guides his decision making. His opinions often focus on the practical effects of a particular decision. For example, one of his criticisms of the *Lopez* ruling was that it "threaten[ed] legal uncertainty in an area of law that . . . seemed reasonably well settled."[60] Although he concurred in the outcome of *Clinton v. Jones* (1997), that the trial for Paula Jones's lawsuit against President Clinton did not have to be postponed until the end of the president's term, Breyer was concerned about possible effects of the trial on the president's abilities to carry out his constitutional responsibilities.

> I concede the possibility that district courts, supervised by the Courts of Appeals and perhaps this Court, might prove able to manage private civil damage actions against sitting Presidents without significantly interfering with the discharge of Presidential duties—at least if they manage those actions with the constitutional problem in mind. Nonetheless, predicting the future is difficult, and I am skeptical.[61]

When the justices invalidated the Line Item Veto Act in *Clinton v. City of New York* (1998), Breyer dissented. "I recognize that the Act before us is novel. [It] represent[s] an experiment that may, or may not, help representative government work better. The Constitution, in my view, authorizes Congress and the President to try novel methods in this way."[62] His dissent from the decision that invalidated the civil damages provision of the Violence Against Women Act contended that the ruling was counterintuitive to the majority's claimed goals. "[T]he Court's complex rules seem unlikely to help secure the very object that they seek, namely, the protection of 'areas of traditional state regulation' from federal intrusion. . . . Complex Commerce Clause rules creating fine distinctions that achieve only random results do little to further the important federalist interests that called them into being."[63]

Summary

In appointing Stephen Breyer to the Supreme Court, President Clinton chose an individual who was viewed by many as a moderate, pragmatic jurist with the ability to build consensus among people with divergent views. His performance on the high court generally has reflected this description. Breyer's pragmatic approach to decision making has led him to support both liberal and conservative case outcomes and to remind his colleagues constantly about the practical results of the Court's decisions. Perhaps the most fitting conclusion is this quotation from his opening statement to the Senate Judiciary Committee.

> I will remember that the decisions I help to make will have an effect upon the lives of many, many Americans, and that fact means that I must do my absolute utmost to see that those decisions reflect both the letter and the spirit of a law that is meant to help them.[64]

CHAPTER SIX

Conclusion

Chapters 2 through 5 focused on the four justices who were nominated and confirmed to the Court since the Bork confirmation controversy in 1987: David Souter, Clarence Thomas, Ruth Bader Ginsburg, and Stephen Breyer. The specific concern was to answer these questions: (1) Were there significant increases in media attention and interest group participation in the nomination and confirmation process after Bork? (2) Were presidents likely to appoint "stealth nominees," who have strong ideological beliefs but who do not have public records that can be used by opponents to block or delay confirmations? Or would they choose judicial moderates who could be confirmed without much controversy? (3) How can one characterize the Supreme Court performance of the new justices? Have they been moderates, or have they demonstrated ideological consistency in either a conservative or liberal direction?

Media Attention and Interest Group Involvement

The Souter nomination in 1990 generated considerable media coverage at least in part because he was a "stealth" candidate being nominated to replace William Brennan, one of the Court's most liberal justices. While many assumed that Souter was a conservative, he did not have a written record that indicated his views on important issues that have come before the Court. In fact, Souter was largely unknown, having served on the federal court of appeals for only three months before President Bush nominated him to the Supreme Court. Thus journalists used much of the time between the nomination announcement and the beginning of the confirmation hearings to obtain information about Souter's background and his political views and judicial philosophy.

The media attention that accompanied the Thomas nomination and confirmation in 1991 was predictable. He was being appointed to succeed Thurgood Marshall, the lone African American justice who had spent his entire career as an advocate for racial equality and social justice. The fact that Thomas, an outspoken African American conservative, was chosen to fill Marshall's seat was viewed by many as an invitation to conflict. In this context, the high level of media attention should have been expected. Thomas's confirmation was the only one that attracted live television coverage by the major television networks, and this was only for the second round of hearings, which focused on Anita Hill's sexual harassment charges.

Ginsburg's nomination in 1993 received somewhat more media attention than might have been anticipated, given that she was viewed as a moderate who could be confirmed easily. She was, however, President Clinton's first nominee to the high court, and she had a distinguished pre-judicial career as the premier litigator on behalf of gender equality. Both of these things made this a high-profile nomination. Of the four, Breyer's nomination in 1994 received the least attention from the media. He, like Ginsburg, was regarded as a moderate, and, because of his prior work as counsel to the Senate Judiciary Committee, he was well respected by senators on both sides of the aisle. In addition, his appointment would not affect the ideological balance on the Court. Consequently, legal experts expected a smooth confirmation for him as well.

The lack of live television coverage by the major networks is not surprising. Although the major networks originally had planned to cover the Bork confirmation proceedings extensively, the hearings themselves did not make for exciting television. As a result, most broadcasters decided to drop their live coverage. An executive producer for CBS news offered this assessment of the situation. "This is intricate, arcane testimony. It's very important. The constitutional issues are at the crux of the ideological battle going on on Capitol Hill. But I don't see the sound bites that allow for coverage."[1]

A recent scholarly analysis offers an in-depth examination of the role of the media in Supreme Court confirmations. In a 1999 article published in the *Journal of Law and Politics,* Michael Comiskey concedes that media attention to Supreme Court nominations and confirmations is much more extensive now than it was a few decades ago. He concludes, however, that claims about the media's role are overblown. Comiskey points to four factors that he says explain the increased media attention. First, he emphasizes the increase in the number of media, including public radio and "politically-oriented talk-radio" programs. "Especially noteworthy," in Comiskey's view, is "the advent of television and the proliferation of channels it carries, including all-news networks, C-Span, public television, and the creation of group-associated cable channels such as the Christian Broadcasting Network, all of which are likely to devote considerable attention to some Supreme

Court confirmation proceedings."[2] Two additional factors include a more aggressive journalistic style and the longer interval between the nomination announcement and the beginning of the confirmation hearings. On this latter point, Comiskey reported that from the Harding through Kennedy administrations, the interval between the nomination and the confirmation vote averaged twenty-three days. By contrast, the interval for Clinton's two noncontroversial appointees, Ginsburg and Breyer, was seven and eleven weeks, respectively.[3] The final factor Comiskey cites in explaining increased media attention is the realization that Supreme Court appointments are important events because the Court increasingly is involved in a tremendous range of important public policy issues.

With respect to interest group involvement in the confirmation process, the Souter and Thomas hearings included testimony from a number of organizations. More than twenty representatives testified in the proceedings for Souter, and nearly fifty organizations were represented during the proceedings for Thomas. Traditional liberal interest groups testified against Souter because of concerns about his positions on important civil rights and liberties issues. Feminist groups particularly feared that he would become the fifth vote to overturn *Roe v. Wade*. Thomas's earlier speeches and writings on various civil rights and liberties issues provoked opposition from a range of interest groups. Given the participation of a number of groups opposing confirmation, organizations in favor of the nomination likely felt compelled to testify on Thomas's behalf. By contrast, fewer than ten groups each testified in the Ginsburg and Breyer hearings.

"Stealth" Nominees or Judicial Moderates?

Some have suggested that a contentious confirmation process is a product of divided government. That is, a confirmation will be more controversial and contentious when the presidency and Senate are controlled by different parties. This conclusion is doubtful. Contentious confirmations appear to be related instead to the president's nomination strategy. It is true that the Bork and Thomas controversies occurred under Republican presidents and Democratic Senates. At the same time, however, Souter also was appointed by a Republican president when the Senate was controlled by Democrats. Under the same political circumstances, Bush chose two different strategies. With Souter, he tried to nominate a "stealth" candidate, one who was conservative but who lacked a written record that could be attacked by opponents. Although there was some Senate opposition to Souter's confirmation, the process itself was not very contentious, at least not in comparison to the Bork nomination. Bush abandoned the "stealth" strategy with the Thomas nomination. There he sought to appoint a very conservative African American nominee by recasting him as a moderate and using Thomas's racial identity to mute opposition from Democrats. While Thomas ultimately was confirmed, the process was long and confrontational.

President Clinton chose a different strategy in his two appointments, even though he had a Democratic Senate. Under those conditions, one might have expected him to appoint liberal nominees, as some of his supporters suggested. He was informed, however, that even though the Democrats were in a majority in the Senate, liberal nominees would have faced a difficult confirmation process. Clinton was unwilling to invest the political capital necessary to get liberal candidates confirmed, so he decided to nominate two well-respected moderates. By doing so, he was able to avoid major confirmation battles in both cases.[4]

Supreme Court Performance

In terms of their performances on the Court, Souter, Ginsburg, and Breyer can be characterized as moderate liberals. Souter began his Supreme Court tenure as a conservative but slowly evolved into a moderate, while Ginsburg and Breyer have been moderate liberals since their arrival on the high court. On a range of issues, including affirmative action, church-state matters, voting rights, abortion, and federalism, these three justices, along with Justice Stevens, have taken consistently liberal positions. They are not, however, liberals in the mold of former Justices Brennan and Marshall who saw the Constitution as a vehicle for bringing about social reform. *Washington Post* reporter Joan Biskupic described the four this way in a 1999 article.

> These four justices are concerned with legal authority, rather than social ideals. They have a broader vision of the Constitution and federal law than the Rehnquist conservatives, to be sure, but rather than expressing an overarching judicial philosophy, they tend to take cases as they come. Pragmatism is their watchword. And unlike both yesterday's liberals—who believed the court should intervene in society's most pressing dilemmas—and today's conservatives—who would consistently prefer to scale back government—these justices generally take the path of least intervention, deciding cases narrowly and avoiding broad mandates.[5]

Thomas, by contrast, has been a consistent member of the conservative bloc on the Court since his first term.

Future Nominations

In light of these recent nominations, Court observers have speculated about the impact of the 2000 presidential election on future Supreme Court appointments.

Specifically, will President George W. Bush try to appoint conservatives, or will he adopt the Clinton strategy of nominating moderates? During the election campaign, Bush named conservative justices Antonin Scalia and Clarence Thomas as the judges he most admired, and he vowed to appoint "strict constructionists" to the Court if elected. In a presidential debate, Bush stated, "The voters will know I'll put competent judges on the bench, people who will strictly interpret the Constitution and will not use the bench to write social policy. I don't believe in liberal, activist judges; I believe in strict constructionists, and those are the kind of judges I will appoint."[6]

It is difficult to know whether he will be able to follow through on this pledge. George W. Bush became president under the most unusual of circumstances. The outcome of the election turned on the winner of Florida's twenty-five electoral votes. On the day after the election, the Florida division of elections announced that Bush had defeated Vice President Al Gore, but because of a narrow margin of victory, Florida law called for an automatic recount of votes in all counties. After the recount, Bush again was declared the winner, but by an even narrower margin. Consistent with Florida law, Gore requested manual recounts in four counties. This put into motion a series of events that eventually led to a United States Supreme Court decision effectively determining Bush to be the winner of the election.

The Supreme Court overturned the Florida Supreme Court's decision ordering a statewide manual recount of previously uninspected undervotes. By a 5–4 vote, the high court ordered an end to the recount, holding that the lack of uniform standards violated the Equal Protection Clause (*Bush v. Gore*, 2000).[7] Voting to halt the recount were Chief Justice Rehnquist and Justices O'Connor, Scalia, Kennedy, and Thomas. Justices Souter and Breyer found an equal protection violation, but they would have remanded the case to the Florida courts with instructions to establish uniform standards for evaluating the ballots. Justices Stevens and Ginsburg did not find an equal protection violation.

The 2000 congressional elections also will have an important impact on potential Supreme Court nominations. The elections initially resulted in a Senate equally divided between Democrats and Republicans, with Vice President Dick Cheney as the potential tie-breaking vote. Under these circumstances, the question was whether Bush would be able to appoint strong conservatives, if he so desired.

Bush's initial actions regarding the federal courts indicate his desire to move in a conservative direction. For example, only two months after taking office, the Bush White House announced that the administration no longer would rely on the ABA Standing Committee on the Federal Judiciary for evaluating candidates for federal judgeships. Administration officials said that they would rely instead on advice from the Federalist Society, an influential conservative legal group that includes among its founders Theodore Olson, appointed by Bush to serve as solicitor general of the United States. Other members include former appellate judge and failed Supreme Court nominee Robert Bork, former independent counsel Kenneth Starr, and a number of prominent federal judges. Many Federalist Society members applauded the announcement regarding the exclusion of the ABA committee from the nomination process. They had been critical of the committee since 1987, when it gave Bork a mixed rating for the Supreme Court. (Ten of fifteen members rated him "well-qualified," four said he was "not qualified," and one person voted "not opposed.") Federalist Society members held the ABA committee at least partly responsible for Bork's defeat.[8]

Senate Judiciary Committee Democrats criticized both the White House's exclusion of the ABA committee and Republican Chairman Orrin Hatch's plan to end a procedure that permits both senators from a nominee's home state to veto a nomination. Senator Patrick Leahy, the Judiciary Committee's ranking Democrat, contended that the Republicans "have dispensed with consultation and quality control checks like peer review, and now they want to stack the deck in the way the Senate handles nominations. It sure looks like they are intent on building an ideologically-driven court-packing machine."[9] Just as Bush pledged during the presidential campaign to appoint "strict constructionists" to the federal judiciary, the Democrats vowed that they would not "rubber-stamp" his nominees.

In early May of 2001, Bush unveiled the list of his first nominees to the federal appellate courts. As expected, the list was dominated by conservatives, including members of the Federalist Society. But Senate dynamics shifted abruptly within a couple of weeks of Bush's first nominations, when Republican Senator Jim Jeffords of Vermont left the party and became an independent. Jeffords joined the Democratic caucus, which gave the Democrats a working majority and, most importantly for federal judicial nominations, control of the Senate Judiciary Committee. Their new majority status emboldened Judiciary Committee Democrats: New York Senator Charles Schumer noted, "The first batch was nominated before the Democrats took power. Now that we're in the majority, I'm sure that the next eleven will not be as conservative. We expect [the Bush administration] to rethink, to recalibrate their political calculations when they send up nominees to us."[10] It also appeared that the shift in control would result in difficult confirmation battles for some of Bush's initial nominees. The confirmation process for Bush's initial nominees was slow, and it became even slower after the terrorist attacks on the World Trade Center and the Pentagon on September 11, 2001.

What do these events portend for the high court? Before the 2000 election, many Court observers anticipated the retirements of Chief Justice Rehnquist and/or Justice O'Connor if Bush became president. They searched in vain for hints about whether the justices indeed would retire at the end of the 2000–2001 term. After the election, however, some scholars and journalists asked whether Rehnquist or O'Connor could retire at the end of that term, given their roles in *Bush v. Gore*. Analysts closely watched the Court near the end of the 2000–2001 term, but no retirement announcement was forthcoming.

If Rehnquist and O'Connor indeed are interested in retiring while the presidency is held by a Republican, the real calculation is in the timing because of the midterm congressional elections in November of 2002. Thirty-six seats will be contested; twenty of these are held by Republicans and fourteen by Democrats. Consequently, Rehnquist and O'Connor will have to decide whether to retire before the congressional elections, even though the Democrats control the Senate by one vote, or wait until after the 2002 elections without knowing which party will be in control. Some also have suggested that if Rehnquist retires first, it might be less difficult to confirm a conservative replacement because a conservative simply would replace a conservative. A conservative nominee to O'Connor's seat clearly would encounter great difficulty being confirmed, because—although she is a conservative—O'Connor has been a swing vote on a number of cases that have had liberal outcomes. Such a nomination would raise concerns about the balance on the Court.

One additional factor that may be important in a Bush nomination is racial and ethnic diversity. Currently no Hispanics serve on the Court, and Bush has indicated a desire to name the first Hispanic justice. The Bush administration views this as an opportunity to increase his support among Hispanic voters for the 2004 presidential election and, in general, to recruit more Hispanics to the Republican Party. Emilio Garza, a conservative federal appeals court judge from Texas, and Alberto Gonzales, Bush's White House counsel, have been mentioned as possible candidates. Both are conservatives. Appointing either of them or some other conservative Hispanic jurist would be similar to his father's strategy in appointing Clarence Thomas.

Final Conclusions

What can be concluded, then, about the impact of the Bork controversy on the Supreme Court nomination and confirmation process since then? It appears that critics have overstated their claim that the Bork episode changed the process forever. The reality is that each nomination is a unique event, with the outcome determined by factors specific to that nomination. The level of media involvement and interest group activity on a nomination, and the types of nominees recommended, depend primarily on the political context in which the nominations arise and on the motives and actions of the appointing president. If a nomination is likely to tip the balance on an evenly divided Court, it is unlikely that strong ideological candidates, whether conservative or liberal, will be confirmed. If presidents desire to avoid bitter and protracted confirmation battles, the safest strategy seems to be the one adopted by President Clinton—selecting well-respected judicial moderates.

Notes

Introduction

1. Henry J. Abraham, *Justices, and Presidents: A Political History of Appointments to the Supreme Court* (New York: Oxford University Press, 1985), 5–6.
2. See John Anthony Maltese, *The Selling of Supreme Court Nominees* (Baltimore: The Johns Hopkins University Press, 1995), 146–147.
3. See Stephen L. Carter, *The Confirmation Mess* (New York: Basic Books, 1994), 191–195.
4. Ibid., 14.
5. Ibid., 17.
6. Ibid., 195–203.
7. Mark Silverstein, *Judicious Choices: The New Politics of Supreme Court Confirmations* (New York: W.W. Norton, 1994), 163.
8. George L. Watson and John A. Stookey, *Shaping America: The Politics of Supreme Court Appointments* (New York: HarperCollins Publishers, 1995), 223.
9. *The Selling of Supreme Court Nominees*, 143.

Chapter 1

1. Janet Blasecki, "Justice Lewis Powell: Swing Voter or Staunch Conservative?" *Journal of Politics* 52 (1990): 530–547.
2. *United States v. Leon,* 468 U.S. 897 (1984), *Milliken v. Bradley,* 418 U.S. 717 (1974), and *San Antonio Independent School District v. Rodriguez,* 411 U.S. 1 (1973).
3. *Plyler v. Doe,* 457 U.S. 202 (1982); *Aguilar v. Felton,* 473 U.S. 402 (1985); and *Booth v. Maryland* 483 U.S. 1056 (1987).
4. See *Roe v. Wade,* 410 U.S. 113 (1973); *Planned Parenthood v. Danforth,* 428 U.S. 52 (1976); *Akron v. Akron Center for Reproductive Health,* 462 U.S. 416 (1983); and *Thornburgh v. American College of Obstetricians and Gynecologists,* 476 U.S. 747 (1986).
5. See *Regents of University of California v. Bakke,* 438 U.S. 265 (1978).
6. Ethan Bronner, *Battle for Justice: How the Bork Nomination Shook America* (New York: W.W. Norton & Company, 1989), 28–30, 32.

7. David M. O'Brien, *Storm Center: The Supreme Court in American Politics*, Fifth Edition (New York: W.W. Norton & Company, 2000), 43.
8. *Battle for Justice*, 31–32.
9. Ibid., 57–71.
10. For further discussion of Bork's explanation of original intent, see his book *The Tempting of America: The Political Seduction of American Law* (New York: Free Press, 1990).
11. See Edwin Meese, "The Battle for the Constitution," *Policy Review* (Spring 1986), 32–35, and William J. Brennan, "The Constitution of the United States: Contemporary Ratification," in *Judges on Judging: Views from the Bench*, edited by David M. O'Brien (Chatham, N.J.: Chatham House, 1997).
12. See Judith Baer, "The Fruitless Search for Original Intention," in Michael McCann and Gerald Houseman, eds., *Judging the Constitution: Critical Essays on Judicial Lawmaking* (Glenview, Ill.: Scott, Forseman, 1989), 63.
13. *Storm Center*, 248.
14. *Battle for Justice*, 83–85, 87–88, 205.
15. Edward M. Kennedy, quoted in *Battle for Justice*, 98.
16. *Battle for Justice*, 50–55, 144–187.
17. Ibid., 191.
18. Ibid., 205–206.
19. *Battle for Justice*, 214.
20. Robert Bork, "Civil Rights–A Challenge," *New Republic*, August 31, 1963, 22.
21. Robert Bork, "Neutral Principles and Some First Amendment Problems," *Indiana Law Journal*, vol. 47, no. 1 (Fall 1971).
22. *Nomination of Judge Robert H. Bork to be Associate Justice of the Supreme Court of the United States: Hearings Before the Senate Committee on the Judiciary*, 100th Cong. (1987), vol. 1, 105.
23. Ibid., 129.
24. Speech at Canisius College, Buffalo, New York, October 8, 1985. Quoted in *Nomination of Judge Robert H. Bork*, vol. 5, 4913.
25. Speech to the Federalist Society, January 31, 1987. Quoted in *Nomination of Judge Robert H. Bork*, vol. 5, 4915.
26. *Nomination of Judge Robert H. Bork*, 104.
27. Ibid., 128–129.
28. Ibid., 130–131.
29. Ibid., 152–154.
30. Ibid., 132–133.
31. Ibid., 115.
32. Ibid., 117.
33. See *Nomination of Judge Bork*, "Bork v. Bork, A Comparison of Judge Bork's Confirmation Testimony with His Previous Speeches and Articles," A Report of the NAACP Legal Defense and Educational Fund, Inc. and People for the American Way Action Fund, September 1987, 4908–4971; "Bork v. Bork, An Analysis of the Bork Record," prepared by the Leadership Conference on Civil Rights, September 1987, 4745–4751.
34. *Storm Center*, 75.
35. *Nomination of Judge Robert H. Bork*, 179.
36. Ibid., 245.
37. For a complete list of witnesses and materials submitted, see *Nomination of Judge Bork*, XXVIII–LII.
38. Thomas R. Hensley, Christopher E. Smith, and Joyce A. Baugh, *The Changing Supreme Court: Constitutional Rights and Liberties* (Minneapolis: West Publishing, 1997), 10–11.

39. *Storm Center*, 77.

40. *The Changing Supreme Court*, 74.

41. *Battle for Justice*, 338.

Chapter 2

1. George H. W. Bush, as quoted in *Washington Post*, July 24, 1990, A. 12.

2. David Garrow, "Justice Souter Emerges," *New York Times Magazine*, September 25, 1994, 64.

3. Henry J. Abraham, *Justices, Presidents, and Senators: A History of the U.S. Supreme Court Appointments from Washington to Clinton* (Lanham, Md: Rowman & Littlefield Publishers, Inc., 1999), 304–305.

4. "Justice Souter Emerges," 36–67.

5. *Webster v. Reproductive Health Services*, 492 U.S. 490 (1989).

6. In *Webster*, the majority upheld provisions of a Missouri statute that (1) prohibited the use of public facilities or employees to perform abortions (2) prohibited public funds from being used for abortion counseling, and (3) required physicians to conduct fetal viability tests before performing abortions. The viability-testing provision was the most controversial because it directly implicated *Roe*. Under *Roe*, regulations that promote fetal life are supposed to be limited to the third trimester of pregnancy, but the viability-testing provision in this statute included the second trimester.

7. *Nomination of David H. Souter to be Associate Justice of the Supreme Court: Hearings Before the Senate Committee on the Judiciary*, 101st Cong. (1990), 51–52.

8. Ibid., 52.

9. Ibid., 70.

10. Ibid., 186.

11. Ruth Marcus, "Senators Left Wondering After Hearing: Which Is the Real David Souter?" *Washington Post*, September 23, 1990, A4.

12. Based on a LEXIS-NEXIS search of general news from the period of July 24–October 2, 1990.

13. Based on a search of Vanderbilt University: Television News Archive and *New York Times*.

14. "Justice Souter Emerges," 41–43.

15. Linda Greenhouse, "An 'Intellectual Mind': David Hackett Souter," *New York Times*, July 24, 1990, A1.

16. Neil A. Lewis, "Liberal Bloc in Turmoil After Souter Encounter," *New York Times*, September 27, 1990, A16.

17. Scott P. Johnson and Christopher E. Smith, "David Souter's First Term on the Supreme Court: the Impact of a New Justice," *Judicature*, 75 (1992): 239.

18. Data extrapolated from Thomas R. Hensley, Christopher E. Smith, and Joyce A. Baugh, *The Changing Supreme Court: Constitutional Rights and Liberties* (St. Paul, Minn.: West Publishing, 1997), 84–86.

19. *Arizona v. Fulminante, 499 U.S. 279 (1991); County of Riverside v. Laughlin, Wilson v. Seiter,* 501 U.S. 294 (1991); *Harmelin v. Michigan*, 501 U.S. 957 (1991); *Mu'min v. Virginia*, 500 U.S. 415 (1991); *Peretz v. United States*, 501 U.S. 923 (1991); and *Schad v. Arizona* 501 U.S. 624 (1991).

20. See John M. Scheb, II and Lee W. Ailshie, "Justice Sandra Day O'Connor and the 'Freshman Effect,'" *Judicature*, 69 (1985): 9–12; Thea F. Rubin and Albert P. Melone, "Justice Antonin Scalia: A First Year Freshman Effect?" *Judicature*, 72 (1988): 98–102; Albert P. Melone. "Revisiting the Freshman Effect Hypothesis: The First Two Terms of Justice Anthony Kennedy," *Judicature*, 74 (1990): 6–13.

21. "David Souter's First Term," 241–242.

22. *Ford v. Georgia* 498 U.S. 411 (1991); *Illinois v. Kentucky* 500 U.S. 380 (1991); *Astoria Federal Savings and Loan Association v. Solimino* 501 U.S. 104 (1991); *Gollust v. Mendell* 499 U.S. 916 (1991); *Yates v. Evatt* 500 U.S. 391 (1991); *James M. Beam Distilling Co. v. Georgia* 501 U.S. 529 (1991); and *Virginia Bankshares Inc. v. Sandberg* 501 U.S. 1083 (1991).

23. *Payne v. Tennessee*, 501 U.S. 808 (1991); overruled were *Booth v. Maryland*, 482 U.S. 496 (1987) and *South Carolina v. Gathers*, 490 U.S. 805 (1989).

24. *Rust v. Sullivan*, 500 U.S. 173 (1991).

25. *Nomination of David H. Souter*, 174.

26. *Barnes v. Glen Theatre, Inc.*, 501 U.S. 560 (1991).

27. *Cohen v. Cowles Media Co.*, 501 U.S. 663, 679 (1991) (Souter, J., dissenting).

28. Data extrapolated from *The Changing Supreme Court*, 84.

29. "Justice Souter Emerges," 64.

30. Data extrapolated from "The Statistics," *The Harvard Law Review*, Volumes 110 (November 1996), 111 (November 1997), 112 (November 1998), 113 (November 1999), and 114 (November 2000).

31. Joan Biskupic, "Court's Quartet of Dissent: Justices Favor Pragmatism Over Liberalism," *Washington Post*, June 27, 1999, A1.

32. *Nomination of David H. Souter*, 115.

33. *Planned Parenthood v. Casey*, 505 U.S. 833 (1992).

34. Ibid., 846.

35. Ibid., 869.

36. *Stenberg v. Carhart*, 530 U.S. 914 (2000).

37. *Lee v. Weisman*, 505 U.S. 577 (1992).

38. Ibid., 627 (Souter, J., concurring).

39. *Rosenberger v. Rector and Visitors of University of Virginia*, 515 U.S.819, 868 (1995) (Souter, J., dissenting).

40. *Agostini v. Felton*, 521 U.S. 203 (1997); *Mitchell v. Helms*, 530 U.S. 793 (2000).

41. *Santa Fe Independent School District v. Doe*, 530 U.S. 290 (2000).

42. *Nomination of David H. Souter*, 432.

43. Ibid., 76.

44. *Faragher v. City of Boca Raton*, 524 U.S. 775, 807 (1998).

45. *Burlington Industries, Inc. v. Ellerth*, 524 U.S. 742 (1998).

46. *Gebser v. Lago Vista Independent School District*, 524 U.S. 274 (1998).

47. See *Regents of the University of California v. Bakke*, 438 U.S. 265 (1978); *United Steelworkers of America v. Weber*, 443 U.S. 193 (1979); *Fullilove v. Klutznick*, 448 U.S. 448 (1980); *Johnson v. Transportation Agency*, 480 U.S. 616 (1987); and *United States v. Paradise*, 480 U.S. 149 (1987).

48. *City of Richmond v. J.A. Croson Co.*, 488 U.S. 469 (1989); *Fullilove v. Klutznick*, 448 U.S. 448 (1979).

49. *Metro Broadcasting Inc. v. F.C.C.*, 497 U.S. 547 (1990).

50. *Nomination of David H. Souter*, 182–183.

51. Ibid., 183–184.

52. *Adarand Constructors, Inc. v. Pena*, 515 U.S. 200, 237 (1995).

53. Ibid., 269 (Souter, J., dissenting).

54. *Shaw v. Reno*, 509 U.S. 630, 680 (1993) (Souter, J., dissenting).

55. *Bush v. Vera*, 517 U.S. 952, 1066 (1996) (Souter, J., dissenting).

56. *Nomination of David H. Souter*, 63.

57. *Garcia v. San Antonio Metropolitan Transit Authority*, 469 U.S. 528 (1985).

58. *National League of Cities v. Usery*, 426 U.S. 833 (1976).

59. *New York v. United States*, 505 U.S. 144 (1992).

60. Ibid., 188.
61. *Printz v. United States*, 521 U.S. 898 (1997).
62. Ibid., 975 (Souter, J., dissenting).
63. *Alden v. Maine*, 527 U.S. 706 (1999).
64. Ibid., 761 (Souter, J., dissenting).
65. *Kimel v. Florida Board of Regents* (2000); *Board of Trustees of the University of Alabama v. Garrett* (2001).
66. *National League of Cities*; *Garcia*.
67. *United States v. Lopez*, 514 U.S. 549 (1995).
68. Ibid., 603 (Souter, J., dissenting).
69. *United States v. Morrison*, 529 U.S. 598, 629 (2000) (Souter, J., dissenting).
70. *Nomination of David H. Souter*, 129.
71. Ibid., 303.
72. *Alden*, 807 (Souter, J., dissenting).
73. *United States v. Thompson/Center Arms Co.*, 504 U.S. 505, 518 (1992).
74. See these articles by Christopher E. Smith for details about Souter's voting behavior in criminal justice cases: "Criminal Justice and the 1995–96 U.S. Supreme Court Term," *University of Detroit Mercy Law Review*, 74 (Fall 1996): 6–9; "Criminal Justice and the 1996–97 U.S. Supreme Court Term," *University of Dayton Law Review*, 23 (Fall 1997): 37–39; "Criminal Justice and the 1997–98 U.S. Supreme Court Term," *Southern Illinois University Law Journal*, 23 (Winter 1998): 450–453; "Criminal Justice and the 1998–99 United States Supreme Court Term," *Widener Journal of Public Law*, 9 (1999): 32–36; "Criminal Justice and the 1999–2000 U.S. Supreme Court Term," *North Dakota Law Review*, 77 (2001): 9–11.
75. *Atwater v. City of Lago Vista*, 121 S.Ct. 1536 (2001).
76. Ibid., 1567 (O'Connor, J., dissenting).
77. *Justices, Presidents, and Senators*, 309.
78. Paul M. Barrett, "Independent Justice: David Souter Emerges as Reflective Moderate on the Supreme Court," *Wall Street Journal*, February 2, 1993, A1.

Chapter 3

1. Christopher E. Smith and Joyce A. Baugh, *The Real Clarence Thomas: Confirmation Veracity Meets Performance Reality* (New York: Peter Lang Publishing, Inc., 2000), 21.
2. *The Real Clarence Thomas*, 15–16; Barbara A. Perry, *The Supremes: Essays on the Current Justices of the Supreme Court of the United States* (New York: Peter Lang Publishing, Inc., 1999), 101–102.
3. *The Supremes*, 102–103.
4. *The Real Clarence Thomas*, 16–17.
5. Ibid., 17.
6. Ibid., 17–18.
7. Ibid., 18.
8. "Excerpts from News Conference Announcing Court Nominee," *New York Times*, July 2, 1991, A14.
9. *Nomination of Judge Clarence Thomas to be Associate Justice of the Supreme Court of the United States: Hearings Before the Committee on the Judiciary, United States Senate*, 102nd Cong., 1st session, pt. 1 (1991), 96.
10. Ibid., 110.
11. Ibid.

12. Ibid., 266.

13. Ibid., 267.

14. *Nomination of Judge Clarence Thomas*, 283.

15. The article Thomas discussed was Lewis Lehrman's, "The Declaration of Independence and the Right to Life: One Leads Unmistakably from the Other," *American Spectator*, April 1987, 21–23.

16. Neil A. Lewis, "The Thomas Nomination: Judiciary Panel Deadlocks, 7–7, on Thomas Nomination to Court," *New York Times*, September 28, 1991, 1.

17. Jane Mayer and Jill Abramson, *Strange Justice: The Selling of Clarence Thomas* (New York: Houghton-Mifflin, 1994), 231–254.

18. *The Real Clarence Thomas*, 25.

19. Ibid., 26.

20. Ibid., 28.

21. Based on a LEXIS-NEXIS search of general news from July 1–October 15, 1991.

22. Based on a search of Vanderbilt University: Television News Archive and *New York Times*.

23. Christopher E. Smith and Scott Patrick Johnson, "The First-Term Performance of Justice Clarence Thomas," *Judicature*, vol. 76, no. 4 (December 1992–January 1993): 174.

24. Data extrapolated from Thomas R. Hensley, Christopher E. Smith, and Joyce A. Baugh, *Supreme Court Update: 2001* (Belmont, Calif.: Wadsworth Publishing, 2001) [to be available online at http://www.wadsworth.com].

25. Data extrapolated from "The Statistics," *The Harvard Law Review*, Volumes 110 (November 1996), 111 (November 1997), 112 (November 1998), 113 (November 1999), and 114 (November 2000).

26. Clarence Thomas, "Affirmative Action Goals and Timetables: Too Tough? Not Tough Enough?" *Yale Law and Policy Review* 5 (1987): 402.

27. *Nomination of Judge Clarence Thomas*, 263.

28. Ibid.

29. *Adarand Constructors, Inc. v. Pena*, 515 U.S. 200, 237 (1995).

30. Ibid., 241 (Thomas, J., concurring).

31. *Nomination of Judge Clarence Thomas*, 410.

32. *Holder v. Hall*, 512 U.S. 874 (1994).

33. Abraham L. Davis and Barbara Luck Graham, *The Supreme Court, Race, and Civil Rights* (Thousand Oaks, Calif.: Sage Publications, 1995), 228.

34. *Holder*, 914 (Thomas, J., concurring).

35. Ibid., 944 (Thomas, J., concurring).

36. *Nomination of Judge Clarence Thomas*, 446.

37. *Shaw v. Reno*, 509 U.S. 630 (1993).

38. *Miller v. Johnson*, 515 U.S. 900 (1995).

39. *Shaw v. Hunt*, 517 U.S. 899 (1996); *Bush v. Vera*, 517 U.S. 952 (1996).

40. *Bush v. Vera*, 1002–1003 (Thomas, J., concurring).

41. *Hunt v. Cromartie*, 121 S.Ct. 1452 (2001).

42. Ibid., 1475 (Thomas, J., dissenting).

43. *United States v. Fordice*, 505 U.S. 717 (1992).

44. Ibid., 749 (Thomas, J., concurring).

45. *Missouri v. Jenkins*, 515 U.S. 70 (1995).

46. Ibid., 114 (Thomas, J., concurring).

47. Ibid.

48. *Planned Parenthood v. Casey*, 505 U.S. 833 (1992).

49. Ibid., 953 (Rehnquist, C.J., concurring and dissenting).
50. Ibid., 980 (Scalia, J., concurring and dissenting).
51. For an explanation of the actual procedure(s) and the development of partial-birth abortion laws, see Karen E. Walther, "Partial Birth Abortion: Should Moral Judgment Prevail Over Medical Judgment?" *Loyola University Chicago Law Journal*, vol. 31 (Summer 2000).
52. *Stenberg v. Carhart*, 530 U.S. 914 (2000).
53. Ibid., 983 (Thomas, J., dissenting).
54. *U.S. Term Limits v. Thornton*, 514 U.S. 779, 837–838 (1995).
55. Ibid., 846 (Thomas, J., dissenting).
56. *Printz v. United States*, 521 U.S. 898, 935 (1997).
57. Ibid., 936–937 (Thomas, J., concurring).
58. *Alden v. Maine*, 527 U.S. 706 (1999).
59. *College Savings Bank v. Florida Prepaid Postsecondary Education Expense Board*, 527 U.S. 666 (1999); *Florida Prepaid Postsecondary Education Expense Board v. College Savings Bank*, 527 U.S. 627 (1999).
60. *Kimel v. Florida Board of Regents*, 528 U.S. 62 (2000); *Board of Trustees of the University of Alabama v. Garrett*, 121 S.Ct. 955 (2001).
61. *Hammer v. Dagenhart*, 247 U.S. 251 (1918).
62. *National League of Cities v. Usery*, 426 U.S. 833 (1976).
63. *United States v. Lopez*, 514 U.S. 549 (1995).
64. Ibid., 585–587 (Thomas, J., concurring).
65. Ibid., 601.
66. *United States v. Morrison*, 529 U.S. 598 (2000).
67. Ibid., 627 (Thomas, J., concurring).
68. *Hudson v. McMillian*, 503 U.S. 1 (1992).
69. Ibid., 28 (Thomas, J., dissenting).
70. *O'Dell v. Netherland*, 521 U.S. 151 (1997); *Jones v. United States*, 527 U.S. 373 (1999).
71. *McFarland v. Scott*, 512 U.S. 849 (1994).
72. Ibid., 856.
73. *Penry v. Johnson.* 121 S.Ct. 1910 (2001).
74. *Shafer v. South Carolina*, 121 S.Ct. 1263 (2001).
75. Ibid., 1276 (Thomas, J., dissenting).
76. *Rosenberger v. University of Virginia*, 515 U.S. 819 (1995).
77. *Mitchell v. Helms*, 120 S.Ct. 2530 (2000).
78. *Good News Club v. Milford Central Schools*, 121 S.Ct. 2093 (2001).
79. *The Real Clarence Thomas*, 50.

Chapter 4

1. Daniel C. Kramer, "Justice Byron R. White: Good Friend to Polity and Solon," in *The Burger Court: Political and Judicial Profiles*, edited by Charles M. Lamb and Stephen C. Halpern (Urbana, Ill.: University of Illinois Press), 407–432.
2. Henry J. Abraham, *Justices, Presidents, and Senators: A History of the U.S. Supreme Court Appointments from Washington to Clinton*, New and Revised Edition (Lanham, Md.: Rowman & Littlefield Publishers, Inc., 1999), 317–318.
3. Kenneth Jost, *The Supreme Court Yearbook: 1992–1993* (Washington, D.C.: CQ Press, 1994), 1.
4. "The Supreme Court," Transcript of President's Announcement and Judge Ginsburg's Remarks, *New York Times*, June 15, 1993, A1.

5. Thomas R. Hensley, Christopher E. Smith, and Joyce A. Baugh, *The Changing Supreme Court: Constitutional Rights and Liberties* (St. Paul, Minn.: West/Wadsworth, 1997), 80.

6. Ibid.

7. Quoted in *Justices, Presidents, and Senators*, 319.

8. *The Changing Supreme Court*, 80.

9. Ibid.

10. Ibid.

11. David A. Kaplan and Bob Kohn, "A Frankfurter, Not a Hot Dog, *Newsweek*, June 28, 1993, 29.

12. *Craig v. Boren*, 429 U.S. 190, 197 (1976).

13. Marcia Coyle, "Nominee's Mettle Will be Tested Soon," *The National Law Journal*, June 28, 1993, 33.

14. *Nomination of Ruth Bader Ginsburg to be Associate Justice of the Supreme Court of the United States: Hearings Before the Senate Committee on the Judiciary*, 103rd Cong. (1993), 51.

15. Ibid., 52.

16. Ibid.

17. *Weisenberger v. Weisenfeld*, 420 U.S. 636 (1975).

18. See Deborah L. Markowitz, "In Pursuit of Equality: One Woman's Work to Change the Law," *Women's Rights Law Reporter*, vol. 11 (Summer 1989): 76.

19. *Nomination of Ruth Bader Ginsburg*, 137.

20. *Planned Parenthood v. Casey*, 505 U.S. 833 (1992).

21. *Roe v. Wade*, 410 U.S. 113 (1973).

22. *Nomination of Ruth Bader Ginsburg*, 149.

23. Ibid., 208.

24. Ibid., 192.

25. Ibid., 265.

26. Based on a LEXIS-NEXIS search of general news from June 14–August 3, 1993.

27. Based on a search of Vanderbilt University: Television News Archive and *New York Times*.

28. Christopher E. Smith, Joyce Ann Baugh, Thomas R. Hensley, and Scott Patrick Johnson, "The First Term Performance of Justice Ruth Bader Ginsburg," *Judicature*, vol. 78, no. 2 (September–October, 1994).

29. Data extrapolated from "The Statistics," *The Harvard Law Review*, Volumes 110 (November 1996), 111 (November 1997), 112 (November 1998), 113 (November 1999), and 114 (November 2000).

30. Data extrapolated from these articles by Christopher E. Smith: "Criminal Justice and the 1995–96 U.S. Supreme Court Term," *University of Detroit Mercy Law Review*, 74 (Fall 1996): 6–9; "Criminal Justice and the 1996–97 U.S. Supreme Court Term," *University of Dayton Law Review*, 23 (Fall 1997): 37–39; "Criminal Justice and the 1997–98 U.S. Supreme Court Term," *Southern Illinois University Law Journal*, 23 (Winter 1998): 450–453; "Criminal Justice and the 1998–99 United States Supreme Court Term," *Widener Journal of Public Law*, 9 (1999): 32–36; "Criminal Justice and the 1999–2000 U.S. Supreme Court Term," *North Dakota Law Review*, 77 (2001): 9–11.

31. *Harris v. Forklift Systems*, 510 U.S. 17 (1993).

32. Ibid., 22.

33. Ibid., 25 (Ginsburg, J., concurring).

34. Ibid., 26.

35. *Oncale v. Sundowner Offshore Services*, 523 U.S. 75 (1998).

36. *Burlington Industries v. Ellerth*, 524 U.S. 742 (1998); *Faragher v. City of Boca Raton* 524 U.S. 775 (1998).

37. *Faragher*, 807.
38. *Gebser v. Lago Vista Independent School District*, 524 U.S. 274 (1998).
39. Ibid., 307 (Ginsburg, J., dissenting).
40. *United States v. Virginia*, 518 U.S. 515, 540 (1996).
41. Ibid., 596 (Scalia, J., dissenting).
42. *Nomination of Ruth Bader Ginsburg*, 164.
43. *United States v. Virginia*, 541–543.
44. *Tuan Anh Nguyen v. INS*, 121 S.Ct. 2053 (2001).
45. Ibid., 2076 (O'Connor, J., dissenting).
46. For a detailed discussion of the actual procedure and the development of partial-birth abortion laws, see Karen E. Walther, "Partial-Birth Abortion: Should Moral Judgment Prevail Over Medical Judgment?" *Loyola University Chicago Law Journal*, vol. 31 (Summer 2000).
47. *Stenberg v. Carhart*, 530 U.S. 914 (2000).
48. Ibid., 951–952 (Ginsburg, J., concurring).
49. *Nomination of Ruth Bader Ginsburg*, 139.
50. Ibid., 140.
51. *Missouri v. Jenkins*, 515 U.S. 70, 176 (1995) (Ginsburg, J., dissenting).
52. *Adarand Constructors, Inc. v. Pena*, 500 U.S. 200, 273–274 (1995) (Ginsburg, J., dissenting).
53. *Romer v. Evans*, 517 U.S. 620 (1996).
54. Ibid., 635.
55. *Callins v. Collins*, 114 S.Ct. 1127, 1130 (1994) (Blackmun, J., dissenting).
56. *Gregg v. Georgia*, 428 U.S. 153 (1976); *Woodson v. North Carolina*, 428 U.S. 280 (1976).
57. *Simmons v. South Carolina*, 512 U.S. 154 (1994).
58. *Romano v. Oklahoma*, 512 U.S. 1 (1994).
59. *Gray v. Netherland*, 518 U.S. 152 (1996).
60. Ibid., 171 (Ginsburg, J., dissenting).
61. *Board of Education of Kiryas Joel v. Grumet*, 512 U.S. 687 (1994)
62. *Rosenberger v. Rector and Visitors of University of Virginia*, 515 U.S. 819 (1995).
63. *Capital Square Review and Advisory Board v. Pinette*, 510 U.S. 1307 (1993).
64. *Santa Fe Independent School District v. Doe*, 530 U.S. 290 (2000).
65. *Mitchell v. Helms*, 530 U.S. 793 (2000).
66. *Good News Club v. Milford Central School*, 121 S. Ct. 2093 (2001).
67. Ibid., 2117 (Souter, J., dissenting).
68. *Nomination of Ruth Bader Ginsburg*, 51.
69. Ibid.
70. *Vernonia School District v. Acton*, 515 U.S. 646 (1995).
71. Ibid., 666 (Ginsburg, J., concurring).
72. *United States v. Alvarez-Sanchez*, 511 U.S. 350 (1994).
73. Ibid., 361 (Ginsburg, J., concurring).
74. *Agostini v. Felton*, 521 U.S. 203 (1997).
75. Ibid., 260 (Ginsburg, J., dissenting).
76. *Adarand*, 271–273 (Ginsburg, J., dissenting).
77. "The Supreme Court: Transcript of President's Announcement and Judge Ginsburg's Remarks," A24.
78. See Joan Biskupic, "Court's Quartet of Dissent: Justices Favor Pragmatism Over Liberalism," *Washington Post*, June 27, 1999, A1.
79. *Nomination of Ruth Bader Ginsburg*, 201.
80. *Nomination of Ruth Bader Ginsburg*, 52.

Chapter 5

1. Kenneth Jost, *The Supreme Court Yearbook: 1993/1994* (Washington, D.C.: Congressional Quarterly, Inc., 1994), 1–2.
2. "Excerpts from Clinton's Remarks Announcing His Selection for Top Court," *The New York Times*, May 14, 1994, 1.
3. *The Supreme Court Yearbook*, 2–3.
4. Tony Mauro, "Not Everyone Happy with the Nomination," *USA Today*, May 16, 1994, 4A.
5. Russell Baker, "Never Be a Nonpareil," *New York Times*, May 17, 1994, A19.
6. "Senate Judiciary Committee: Initial Questionnaire (Supreme Court)," *Nomination of Stephen G. Breyer to be an Associate Justice of the Supreme Court of the United States: Hearings before the Committee on the Judiciary*, 103rd Cong. (1994), 23–24; *The Supreme Court Yearbook*, 3–4.
7. *Nomination of Stephen G. Breyer*, 24–25.
8. *The Supreme Court Yearbook*, 4–5.
9. *Nomination of Stephen G. Breyer*, 20–21.
10. Ibid., 201.
11. Stephen G. Breyer, *Breaking the Vicious Circle: Toward Effective Risk Regulation* (Cambridge: Harvard University Press, 1993).
12. *Nomination of Stephen G. Breyer*, 116.
13. Ibid., 128.
14. Ibid., 145.
15. Ibid., 392–394.
16. Based on a LEXIS-NEXIS search of general news from May 13–July 19, 1994.
17. Based on a search of Vanderbilt University: Television News Archive and *New York Times*.
18. Christopher E. Smith, Joyce A. Baugh, and Thomas R. Hensley, "The First-Term Performance of Justice Stephen Breyer," *Judicature*, vol. 79, no. 2 (September–October): 75–76.
19. Data extrapolated from "The Statistics," *The Harvard Law Review*, Volumes 110 (November 1996), 111 (November 1997), 112 (November 1998), 113 (November 1999), and 114 (November 2000).
20. Data extrapolated from these articles by Christopher E. Smith: "Criminal Justice and the 1995–96 U.S. Supreme Court Term," *University of Detroit Mercy Law Review*, 74 (Fall 1996): 6–9; "Criminal Justice and the 1996–97 U.S. Supreme Court Term," *University of Dayton Law Review*, 23 (Fall 1997): 37–39; "Criminal Justice and the 1997–98 U.S. Supreme Court Term," *Southern Illinois University Law Journal*, 23 (Winter 1998): 450–453; "Criminal Justice and the 1998–99 United States Supreme Court Term," *Widener Journal of Public Law*, 9 (1999): 32–36; "Criminal Justice and the 1999–2000 U.S. Supreme Court Term," *North Dakota Law Review*, 77 (2001): 9–11.
21. *Planned Parenthood v. Casey*, 505 U.S. 833, 943 (1992) (Blackmun, J., concurring in part/dissenting in part).
22. *Rust v. Sullivan*, 500 U.S. 173 (1991).
23. For further details of the procedure and the development of partial-birth abortion statutes, see Karen E. Walther, "Partial-Birth Abortion: Should Moral Judgment Prevail Over Medical Judgment?" *Loyola University Chicago Law Journal*, vol. 31 (Summer 2000).
24. *Stenberg v. Carhart*, 530 U.S. 914 (2000).
25. The primary issue revolved around analysis of the most common procedure for performing second trimester abortions, dilation and evacuation. D&E, as it is most commonly known, involves dilating the cervix, removing some fetal tissue using nonvacuum surgical instruments, and the potential need for instrumental dismemberment of the fetus or the collapse of fetal

parts to facilitate evacuation from the uterus. Such dismemberment typically occurs as the doctor pulls a portion of the fetus through the cervix into the birth canal. According to some physicians, this D&E procedure poses significantly lower risks than the next safest procedure for mid-second trimester abortions. After the 16th week of pregnancy, a variation of D&E is sometimes used. This procedure, referred to as intact D&E, involves removing the fetus from the uterus in one pass, and it can be done in one of two ways, depending upon whether the fetus presents head first or feet first. The feet-first method, referred to as D&X (dilation and extraction), is the procedure most associated with the term "partial birth abortion." This is the procedure used by the physician who challenged the Nebraska law. Breyer accepted the district court's finding that despite disagreements over whether D&X is generally safer than other procedures, D&X "obviates health risks in some circumstances," and therefore, the law requires a health exception. In the majority's view, the statutory language was so vague that it threatened more than the so-called partial birth abortions. Specifically, the statute's language regarding "intentionally delivering into the vagina a living fetus or a substantial portion thereof" did not distinguish between the D&E and D&X procedures. Breyer said that "both procedures can involve the introduction of a 'substantial portion' of a still-living fetus, through the cervix, into the vagina—the very feature of an abortion that leads to characterizing such a procedure as involving 'partial birth.'" Although the state's attorney general contended that his interpretation of the statute did in fact differentiate between the two procedures, the Court rejected his argument, holding that it conflicted with the language in the statute. Breyer concluded that because all those who perform abortion procedures using the D&E method must fear prosecution, conviction, and imprisonment, the Nebraska law imposes an undue burden upon a woman's right to make an abortion decision.

26. *Rosenberger v. Rector and Visitors of the University of Virginia*, 515 U.S. 819 (1995).
27. Ibid., 863 (Souter, J., dissenting).
28. *Santa Fe Independent School District v. Doe*, 530 U.S. 290, 310 (2000).
29. *Mitchell v. Helms*, 530 U.S. 793 (2000).
30. Ibid., 839 (O'Connor, J., concurring in the judgment).
31. *Good News Club v. Milford Central School*, 121 S.Ct. 2093 (2001).
32. *Ibid*, 2111 (Breyer, J., concurring in part).
33. *Denver Area Educational Telecommunications Consortium v. Federal Communications Commission*, 518 U.S. 727 (1996).
34. Ibid., 732.
35. *Reno v. American Civil Liberties Union*, 521 U.S. 844 (1997).
36. *United States v. Playboy Entertainment Group, Inc.*, 529 U.S. 803 (2000).
37. Ibid., 847 (Breyer, J., dissenting).
38. *Colorado Republican Federal Campaign Committee v. Federal Election Commission*, 518 U.S. 604 (1996).
39. Ibid., 615.
40. *Nixon v. Shrink Missouri Government PAC*, 528 U.S. 377, 401 (2000) (Breyer, J., concurring).
41. *FEC v. Colorado Republican Federal Campaign Committee*, 121 S.Ct. 2351 (2001).
42. *Shaw v. Reno*, 509 U.S. 630 (1993).
43. *Miller v. Johnson*, 515 U.S. 900 (1995).
44. *Shaw v. Hunt*, 517 U.S. 899 (1996); *Bush v. Vera*, 517 U.S. 952 (1996).
45. *Abrams v. Johnson*, 521 U.S. 74 (1997).
46. Ibid., 119 (Breyer, J., dissenting).
47. *Hunt v. Cromartie*, 121 S.Ct. 1452 (2001).
48. *United States v. Lopez*, 514 U.S. 549 (1995).

49. Ibid., 623 (Breyer, J., dissenting).
50. *United States v. Morrison*, 529 U.S. 598, 617.
51. Ibid., 656 (Breyer, J., dissenting).
52. *Printz v. United States*, 521 U.S. 898, 935 (1997).
53. Ibid., 977 (Breyer, J., dissenting).
54. *Alden v. Maine*, 527 U.S. 706 (1999).
55. *Seminole Tribe v. Florida*, 517 U.S. 44 (1996).
56. *Board of Trustees of the University of Alabama v. Garrett*, 121 S.Ct. 955, 967–968.
57. Ibid., 970 (Breyer, J., dissenting).
58. *Nomination of Stephen G. Breyer*, 231.
59. Ibid., 287.
60. *Lopez* (Breyer, J., dissenting).
61. *Clinton v. Jones*, 520 U.S. 681, 723 (1997) (Breyer, J., concurring in the judgment).
62. *Clinton v. City of New York*, 524 U.S. 417, 496–497 (1998) (Breyer, J., dissenting).
63. *United States v. Morrison*, 529 U.S. 598, 658 (Breyer, J., dissenting).
64. *Nomination of Stephen G. Breyer*, 21.

Chapter 6

1. "Bork Drama: Long on Exposition, Short on Action," *Broadcasting*, September 21, 1987, p. 36.
2. Michael Comiskey, "Not Guilty: The News Media in the Supreme Court Confirmation Process," *Journal of Law & Politics*, 15 (Winter 1999): 8.
3. Ibid., 12.
4. See John Anthony Maltese, *The Selling of Supreme Court Nominees* (Baltimore: The Johns Hopkins University Press, 1995); George L. Watson and John A. Stookey, *Shaping America: The Politics of Supreme Court Appointments* (New York: HarperCollins Publishers, 1995); Mark Silverstein, *Judicious Choices: The New Politics of Supreme Court Confirmations* (New York: W.W. Norton, 1994); Karen O'Connor and Barbara Palmer, "The Clinton Clones: Ginsburg, Breyer, and the Clinton Legacy," *Judicature* 84 (March/April 2001): 262–273; and Bryon J. Moraski and Charles R. Shipan, "The Politics of Supreme Court Nominations: A Theory of Institutional Constraints and Choices," *American Journal of Political Science*, 43 (October 1999): 1069–1095.
5. Joan Biskupic, "Court's Quartet of Dissent: Justices Favor Pragmatism Over Liberalism," *Washington Post*, June 27, 1999, A1.
6. Neil A. Lewis, "The 2000 Campaign: The Judiciary; Presidential Candidates Differ Sharply on Judges They Would Appoint to Top Courts," *New York Times*, October 8, 2000, 28. Section 1.
7. *Bush v. Gore*, 531 U.S. 98 (2000).
8. Neil A. Lewis, "A Conservative Legal Group Thrives in Bush's Washington," *New York Times*, April 18, 2001, A1.
9. Thomas B. Edsall, "Democrats Press Bush for Input on Judges: Court Nominees Concern Senators," *Washington Post*, April 28, 2001, A4.
10. Neil A. Lewis, "Washington Talk: Road to Federal Bench Gets Bumpier in Senate," *New York Times*, June 26, 2001, A16.

Name/Subject Index

ABC, 22, 46, 68, 87
ABC News Nightline, 22, 46, 68, 87
abortion, 6, 28–29, 44, 53–54, 66, 73, 89–90
Abraham, H., 1
affirmative action, 31, 32, 40, 49, 50, 61, 74, 95
AFL-CIO, 10, 47
Age Discrimination in Employment Act, 35, 56
Agudath Israel of America, 48
Alliance for Justice, 22, 24, 47, 69
American Association of University Women, 47
American Bar Association's Standing Commit-
    tee on the Federal Judiciary, 10, 19, 23,
    47, 48, 68, 69, 83, 87, 105
American Civil Liberties Union, 10, 24
Americans for Democratic Action, 47
Americans United for Life, 69, 87
Americans with Disabilities Act, 35, 56, 98
Anderson, C., 41
Anderson, M., 41
Arnold, R., 81, 87
Association of the Bar of the City of New York,
    69, 87
Atwater, G., 38

Babbitt, B., 62, 81, 87
Bader, C., 63
Bader, N., 63
Baird, Z., 82, 86
Baker, H., 7
Baltimore Sun, The, 87
Berger, V., 65
Biden, J., 11, 14, 15, 37, 45, 49, 84, 86

Biskupic, J., 27, 104
Blackmun, H., 24, 26, 27, 28, 49, 58, 70, 82
    and abortion rights, 67, 89
    and the death penalty, 76
    retirement of, 81
Blasecki, J., 6
Bork, R., 1, 6–17, 22, 36, 42, 46, 60, 66, 68, 87,
    101, 103, 106, 107
    background of, 7–9
    "confirmation conversion of," 15
    confirmation hearings, 11–15
        approval of, 86
    constitutional interpretation, 11, 12
    controversy over nomination, 2, 4
        details of hearing, 4
        early controversy, 9–10
        impact on future appointments, 4
        second controversy, 16–17
    final confirmation vote, 16
    nomination of, 7
Boston Globe, 21, 68, 87
Brandeis, L., 3
Brady Handgun Violence Prevention Act of
    1993, 34, 35, 55, 97
Breaking the Vicious Cycle (Breyer), 84
Brennan, W., 8, 21, 22, 25, 27, 32, 39, 40, 69, 80,
    81
    and capital punishment, 75
    retirement of, 18
Breyer, S., 1, 4, 19, 27, 36, 52, 53, 59, 62, 81–100,
    101
    and abortion rights, 73

Breyer, S *(cont'd)*
  background, 82–83
  call for consensus in judicial decision mak-
    ing, 84
  confirmation hearings, 83–86
  and economics, 85
  and Hispanic organizations, 82
  judicial performance, 88–100
    abortion, 89–90
    cable television/Internet/political speech,
      92–95
    church-state issues, 91–92
    civil rights, 95–96
    commerce power and federalism, 96–99
    judicial philosophy, 99–100
    voting behavior, 88–89
  interest group participation in confirmation
    proceedings, 87–88
  media coverage of nomination proceedings,
    86–87, 102
Bronner, E., 17
Burger, W., 6, 81
Bush, President G. W., 1, 4, 105, 106, 107
Bush, President George H. W., 18, 19, 21, 40,
  42, 60, 101
Business Week, 21

cable television, 92–95
California Women Lawyers, 24, 69
campaign funding, 94
capital sentencing proceedings, 58
Carter, President J., 42, 61, 64, 83
Carter, S., 2
CBS, 22, 46, 68, 87, 102
Center for Constitutional Rights, 23, 47
Cheney, D., 4, 105
Christian Broadcasting Network, 102
church-state issues, 29–30, 59, 77–78, 91, 92
Citizens for God and Country, 24
Citizens for Law and Order, 48
civil rights, 30–33, 49–53, 61, 95–96
Civil Rights Act of 1964, 11, 14
  public accommodations provisions of, 13
Clinton, President W., 61, 68, 80, 81, 87, 99,
  100, 102, 104, 108
  and abortion rights, 62, 90
  nomination of Breyer, 82
  nomination of Ginsburg, 62
CNN, 22, 46, 87

Coalition of Bar Associations of Color, 88
Coalition of Black Trade Unionists, 47
Coalition for America, 24
College of the Holy Cross, 41
Columbia Law School, 64, 65
Columbia University, 63
Comiskey, M., 102
Commerce Clause, 35, 36, 57, 96, 97, 100
commerce powers, 35–36
Communications Decency Act of 1996, 93
Concerned Women for America, 48
Confirmation Mess, The (Carter), 2
confirmation process for Supreme Court
    justices
  media influence of, 2
  politicization of, 1, 2, 17
  support of, 3
Congressional Quarterly, 25
Conservative Caucus, Inc., 23, 69
Council of 100, 48
Cornell University, 16, 63
Court TV, 46, 68
Cox, A., 9
Cruel and Unusual Punishment Clause, 58–59
C-SPAN, 46, 68, 87, 102
Culvahouse, A. B., 7
Cuomo, M., 62

D'Amato, A., 65
Danforth, J., 41, 43
death benefits, 66
death penalty, 40, 57, 58, 67
DeConcini, D., 36
Department of Education, 42
Dole, R., 65
Douglas, W. O., 7, 15
dual federalism, 55

Eagle Forum, 69
Economist, The, 21
Eighth Amendment, 57, 58
Elementary and Secondary Education Act, 79
Eleventh Amendment, 35
Environmental Protection Agency, 85
Equal Employment Opportunity Commission,
  42
Equal Protection Clause, 6, 14, 30, 33, 36, 62,
  72, 105
Establishment Clause, 29, 59, 61, 77, 79, 91, 92

Fair Labor Standards Act, 34, 35, 55, 56, 98
Family Research Council, 69
federal affirmative action programs, 79
Federal Child Labor Act, 56
Federal Communications Commission, 32
Federal Election Commission, 94
Federal Rules of Civil Procedure, 79
federalism, 33–35, 54–57, 97–98
Federalist Society, 12, 105, 106
Feinstein, D., 65
First Amendment, 92, 93, 94
Ford, President G., 7, 16
Fortas, A., 2
Fourth Amendment exclusionary rule, 6, 38, 78
Fourteenth Amendment, 30, 32, 34, 37, 62, 67, 98
Frankfurter, F, 38
    and Ginsburg, 63
Fraternal Order of Police, 24
Free Congress Foundation, 27
Fund for the Feminist Majority, 23, 47
future nominations to the Supreme Court,
    104–7

"gag rule," 26, 89
Garza, E., 107
gender discrimination litigation, 64
Ginsburg, D., 16–17
Ginsburg, M., 63
Ginsburg, R. B., 4, 27, 31, 62, 81, 84, 87, 88, 101
    background, 63–65
    church-state issues, 77–78
    confirmation of, 68
    confirmation politics, 65–68
    criticism of Roe v. Wade, 62
    and death benefits, 66
    and death penalty, 67, 75–77
        sentencing phase, 76
    and gender discrimination litigation, 64
    and government accommodation, 91
    habeas corpus, 76–77
    interest group participation in confirmation
        proceedings, 69
    judicial performance, 69–80
        abortion rights, 73
        affirmative action, 74
        gender discrimination, 71–73, 75
        racial discrimination, 73–74
        school segregation, 74
        voting behavior, 70

media coverage of confirmation proceedings,
    68, 102
and New Jersey Civil Liberties Union, 64
and Stephen Weisenfeld, 66
support for abortion rights, 62, 66
Goldberg, A., 83
Goldwater, B., 8
Gonzales, A., 107
Good News Club, 59
Gore, A., 105
Greenhouse, L., 22
Griscom, T., 7
gun control, 55, 56
Gun Free School Zones Act of 1990, 35, 36, 56,
    96

Hamilton, A., 34, 65
Harvard College, 19
Harvard Law Review, 27, 49, 70, 88, 89
Harvard Law School, 16, 17, 19, 63, 83
Hatch, O., 15, 21, 45, 65, 67, 82, 99, 106
Hayes, President R. B., 3
Haynesworth, C. Jr., 3
Heartland Coalition, 48
Helms, J., 68
Hernandez, A., 30
"high-tech lynching," 45
Hill, A., 44, 65, 102
    Clarence Thomas hearings, 44–46
    media coverage, 46
Hispanic National Bar Association, 23, 69, 82,
    88
Home School Legal Defense Association, 87
Hoover, President H., 3
Hughes, C. E., 3

Indiana Law Journal, 11, 14
interest groups
    and Breyer confirmation proceedings, 87–88
    and Ginsburg confirmation proceedings, 69
    and Souter confirmation proceedings, 22–24
    and Thomas confirmation proceedings, 46–
        48
International Association of Chiefs of Police,
    23, 48
International Narcotics Enforcement Officers
    Association, 24
Internet, 92–95
interstate commerce, 56

Jeffords, J., 4–5, 106
Jipping, T., 27
Johnson, President L., 2, 61
Jones, P., 99
Journal of Law and Politics, 102
judicial restraint, 78
Judicial Selection Monitoring Project, 69
*Judicious Choices: The New Politics of Supreme
    Court Confirmations* (Silverstein), 2

Kansas City Metropolitan School District, 74
Kennedy, A., 16, 17, 19, 21, 25, 29, 52, 70, 88, 96
    on abortion, 53, 89
    and gender discrimination, 75
    and government accommodation, 91
    and television regulation, 93
Kennedy, E., 9, 13, 14, 15, 21, 51, 73, 82, 85
Kennedy, J. F., 61
Ku Klux Klan, 77
Kohl, H., 43

Lambda Legal Defense and Education Fund, 23
Law Review, 63
Lawyers' Committee for Civil Rights Under
    Law, 46
Leadership Conference for Civil Rights, 10, 22,
    24, 30, 47, 69
Leahy, P., 15, 44, 106
Line Item Veto Act, 99
Lloyd's of London, 86
Low-Level Radioactive Waste Policy Amend-
    ments Act of 1985, 34
Los Angeles Times, 21, 68, 87

Magdalen College, Oxford University, 82
March for Life Education and Defense Fund, 69
Marshall, T., 26, 27, 42, 60, 61, 69, 80, 81, 102
    and capital punishment, 75
    retirement of, 40
Matthews, S., 3
Maltese, J. A., 3, 4
media coverage
    of Breyer confirmation proceedings, 86–87
    of Ginsburg confirmation proceedings, 68
    of Souter confirmation proceedings, 21–22
    of Thomas confirmation proceedings, 46
media influence of confirmation process, 2
Meese, E., 7, 8
Metzenbaum, H., 21, 28, 67, 85

Mexican-American Legal Defense and Educa-
    tion Fund, 23, 30, 47
Miami Herald, 68, 87
Minneapolis Star Tribune, 68, 87
Mitchell, G., 81
Monsanto Chemical Company, 42
Montgomery County (Maryland) Black Re-
    publican Council, 48
Moseley-Braun, C., 65
Mothers Against Drunk Driving, 23
Moynihan, D. P., 65

NAACP Legal Defense and Educational Fund,
    10, 40, 47
Nader, R., 82
National Abortion Rights Action League, 23, 47
National Asian Pacific-American Bar Associa-
    tion, 47, 69, 88
National Association for the Advancement of
    Colored People (NAACP), 24, 47
National Association of Criminal Defense Law-
    yers, 24, 47
National Association of Women Judges, 24
National Baptist Convention, U.S.A., Inc., 47
National Bar Association, 47, 88
National Black Nurses Association, 48
National Black Police Association, 47
National Black Women's Health Project, 47
National Center for Neighborhood Enterprise,
    48
National Code of Prison Regulation, 58
National Conference of Black Lawyers, 47
National Council of Churches, 10
National Council of Jewish Women, 23
National Council of La Raza, 10
National Council of Senior Citizens, 47
National Education Association, 10
National Firearms Act, 37
National Gay and Lesbian Task Force, 23
National Law Enforcement Council, 48
National Lawyers' Guild, 23
National Organization for Women, 10, 17, 23,
    47
National Public Radio (NPR), 44
National Republican Senatorial Committee, 94
National Sheriffs Association, 24, 48
National Troopers Coalition, 24, 48
National Women's Law Center, 24, 46
National Women's Political Caucus, 47

Native American Bar Association, 88
NBC, 22, 46, 68, 87
Neas, R., 9
New Hampshire Bar Association, 23
New Jersey American Civil Liberties Union, 64
New Progressives, 3
New Republic, 11
New Right, 3
New York Times, 21, 22, 25, 68, 87
Newsweek, 21
Nickles, D., 68
Nixon, President R., 9
Norton, E. H., 65
NOW Legal Defense and Education Fund, 23, 47

O'Connor, S. D., 1, 19, 25, 26, 34, 49, 51, 59, 70,
    71, 73, 79, 88, 92, 96
  on abortion, 53, 89
  and government accommodation, 91
Office for Civil Rights (DOE), 42
Olson, T., 106
"original intent jurisprudence," 60
Oxford University, 19, 83

Palmieri, E., 63
Parker, J., 3
parochial aid, 79
"partial birth abortion," 29, 53, 73, 90
PBS, 22, 46, 68, 87
People for the American Way, 10, 24, 47
Planned Parenthood, 23, 47
political speech, 92–95
politicization of confirmation process,. *See* con-
    firmation process
Powell, L., 6, 21
Professional Bail Agents, 48
Progressive National Baptist Convention, 47
Public Citizen's Health Research Group, 88

racial discrimination, 74
racial gerrymander, 52, 95
random drug testing, 78
Rath, T., 39
Rauh, J., 30
Reagan, President R., 1, 7, 9, 16, 42
redistricting, 33, 51, 52, 95
Rehnquist, W., 1, 7, 19, 25, 28, 35, 48, 49, 51, 52,
    54, 96, 97
  on abortion, 53, 90

and capital sentencing proceedings, 58
and church-state issues, 59
and government accommodation, 91
and school desegregation, 74
Republican Black Caucus, 48
Reynolds, W. B., 7
Richardson, E., 9
Riley, R., 62
Ruckelshaus, W., 9
Rudman, W., 19
Rutgers University, 63
Rutledge, J., 3

safe harbor rule, 78
San Diego Union-Tribune, 21
San Francisco Chronicle, 21, 68
"Saturday Night Massacre," 9
Scalia, A., 7, 19, 25, 28, 31, 37, 38, 48, 49, 52, 96,
    97, 105
  on abortion, 53, 54, 90
  and church-state issues, 59
  and death penalty, 58
  and gender discrimination, 72
  and government accommodation, 91
school desegregation, 52
school prayer, 77
school segregation, 74, 95
school-sponsored prayer, 59
Schumer, C., 106
Selling of Supreme Court Nominees, The (Mal-
    tese), 3
Senate Judiciary Committee, 5, 16, 20, 38, 43,
    46, 65, 80, 82, 83, 87, 100, 102, 106
sexual harassment, 31, 71
*Shaping America: The Politics of Supreme Court
    Appointments* (Watson & Stookey), 3
Silverstein, M., 2, 3
Simpson, A., 15, 45
Smith, R., 68
Society of American Law Teachers, 24, 46
Souter, D., 4, 18–39, 42, 46, 53, 60, 69, 70, 79,
    87, 97, 101, 103
  background of, 19, 20
  confirmation politics, 19–21, 61
  and death penalty, 76
  and government accommodation, 91
  judicial performance, 24–38
    abortion, 28–29, 89
    church-state issues, 29–30

Souter, D. (cont'd)
    civil rights and liberties issues, 25, 30–33
    commerce powers, 35–36
    conservative voting record, 25
    federalism, 33–35
    general judicial philosophy, 36–38
    interest groups and confirmation proceed-
        ings, 22–24
    media coverage of confirmation proceedings,
        21–22, 101
    and the Robert Bork controversy, 18
    voting statistics, 27
Southeastern Legal Foundation, 24
Specter, A., 45, 67
Stanford University, 16, 82
Starr, K., 106
state immunity, 56
St. Louis Post-Dispatch, 21, 68, 87
St. Petersburg Times, 21
"stealth" candidate, 18, 38, 101, 103–4
Stevens, J. P. 1, 7, 27, 28, 34, 49, 54, 70, 88
    and death penalty, 76
    and government accommodation, 91
    and school prayer, 77
Stookey, J., 3
student-led prayer in public schools, 91
Sununu, J., 18, 19, 27
Supreme Court justices
    recommended term limits, 2
Supreme Court Watch, 23, 47

Tenth Amendment, 34, 35, 54, 55
Thomas, C., 1, 4, 28, 40–60, 66, 68, 86, 87, 88,
        96, 101, 103, 104, 105, 107
    on abortion, 44
    and Anita Hill, 44, 45–46, 65
    background of, 41
    and civil rights and racial equality, 40
    confirmation politics, 42–46, 61, 86
        details of hearing, 43
        outcome of vote, 46
    and government accommodation, 91
    interest group participation, 46–48, 103
    judicial performance, 48–60
        abortion, 53–54
        capital sentencing proceedings, 58
        church-state issues, 59
        civil rights, 49–53
        criminal justice, 57–59

        death penalty, 57, 58
        federalism and commerce powers, 54–57
        general judicial philosophy, 60
        redistricting, 51, 52
        school desegregation, 52
        voting behavior, 48–49
    media coverage, 46, 102
    "original intent jurisprudence," 60
Thomas, M. C., 41
Thurmond, S., 12, 13, 34, 67
Twentieth Century Fund
    suggested reform of confirmation process, 2

United Auto Workers, 10
United States Sentencing Commission, 83
University of Chicago, 8
University of Chicago Law School, 8, 16
Urban League, 10
U.S. News and World Report, 21

Violence Against Women Act of 1994, 36, 57,
        97, 100
Virginia Military Institute, 30, 72
voting rights, 50
Voting Rights Act of 1965, 50, 51

Wall Street Journal, 21, 68, 87
Warren, E., 53
Washington, G., 1, 3
Washington Legal Foundation, 48
Washington Post, 21, 27, 68, 87, 104
Watergate Special Prosecutor Commission, 83
Watson, G., 3
Weisenfeld, S., 66, 69
White, B., 19, 25, 26, 28, 80
    and abortion, 61
    and affirmative action, 61
    retirement of, 61
"white flight," 53
Williams, L., 41
Wilson, President W., 3
Women's Legal Defense Fund, 24, 46
Women's Rights Project, 64
World Trade Center, 106
Wulf, M., 64

Yale Law School, 8, 9, 41

Zeta Phi Beta Sorority, Inc., 48

Court Case Index

Abrams v. Johnson, 95
Adarand Constructors, Inc. v. Pena, 32, 49, 52, 74, 79
Agostini v. Felton, 30, 79
Aguilar v. Felton, 79
Akron v. Akron Center for Reproductive Health, 28
Alden v. Maine, 35, 37, 55, 98
Atwater v. City of Lago Vista, 38

Barnes v. Glen Theatre, Inc., 26
Board of Kiryas Joel v. Grumet, 77
Board of Trustees of the University of Alabama v. Garrett, 35, 98
Brown v. Board of Education, 37, 53
Buckley v. Valeo, 94
Burlington Industries, Inc. v. Ellerth, 31, 71
Bush v. Gore, 105, 107
Bush v. Vera, 33, 51, 95

Capital Square Review and Advisory Board v. Pinette, 77
City of Richmond v. Croson, 31, 79
Clinton v. City of New York, 99
Clinton v. Jones, 99
Cohen v. Cowles Media Co., 26
Colorado Republican Federal Campaign Committee v. Federal Election Commission, 94
Craig v. Boren, 64

Denver Area Educational Telecommunications

Consortium v. Federal Communications Commission, 93

Faragher v. Boca Raton, 31, 71
FEC v. Colorado Republican Federal Campaign Committee, 95
Federal Communications Commission v. Pacifica Foundation, 93
Frontiero v. Richardson, 64, 66

Garcia v. San Antonio Metropolitan Transit Authority, 34, 56
Gebser v. Lago Vista Independent School District, 31, 71
Good News Club v. Milford Central School, 59, 78, 92
Gray v. Netherland, 76
Griswold v. Connecticut, 11, 14, 15, 83

Harris v. Forklift Systems, 71
Helling v. McKinney, 58
Holder v. Hall, 50
Hudson v. McMillian, 58
Hunt v. Cromartie, 52, 96

Kimel v. Florida Board of Regents, 35

Lee v. Weisman, 29, 59

McFarland v. Scott, 58
Metro Broadcasting v. FCC, 32, 50, 79
Miller v. Johnson, 95

Missouri v. Jenkins, 52, 74
Mitchell v. Helms, 30, 59, 91
Mobile v. Bolden, 50

National League of Cities v. Usery, 34, 56
New York v. United States, 34
Nixon v. Shrink Missouri Government PAC, 94

Payne v. Tennessee, 25
Penry v. Johnson, 58
Planned Parenthood v. Casey, 28, 29, 53, 66, 73, 89, 90
Printz v. United States, 34, 55, 97

Reed v. Reed, 64, 66, 72
Reno v. ACLU, 93
Roe v. Wade, 6, 19, 22, 23, 28, 29, 44, 62, 66, 73, 81, 90, 103
Romano v. Oklahoma, 76
Romer v. Evans, 30, 75
Rosenberger v. University of Virginia, 30, 59, 77, 91
Rust v. Sullivan, 26, 28, 89

Santa Fe Independent School District v. Doe, 30, 59, 77, 91

Seminole Tribe of Fla v. Florida, 35, 98
Shafer v. South Carolina, 58
Shaw v. Hunt, 33, 51, 95
Shaw v. Reno, 33, 51, 95
Simmons v. South Carolina, 76
Stenberg v. Carhart, 29, 53, 73

Thornburgh v. American College of Obstetricians and Gynecologists, 28
Thornburgh v. Gingles, 50, 51

United States v. Alvarez-Sanchez, 78
United States v. Fordice, 52
United States v. Lopez, 35, 56, 96
United States v. Morrison, 57, 97
United States v. Playboy Entertainment Group, Inc., 93
United States v. Virginia, 30, 71, 72
U.S. Term Limits v. Thornton, 54, 55

Vernonia School District v. Acton, 78

Webster v. Reproductive Health Services, 19
Weinberger v. Weisenfeld, 66, 69
White v. Regester, 50, 51